WELCOME TO
KINDERGARTEN

WELCOME TO KINDERGARTEN

A Month-by-Month Guide to Teaching and Learning

**Bonnie Brown Walmsley
& Debra Redlo Wing**

FOREWORD BY
LILIAN G. KATZ

HEINEMANN
Portsmouth, NH

Heinemann
A division of Reed Elsevier Inc.
361 Hanover Street
Portsmouth, NH 03801–3912
www.heinemann.com

Offices and agents throughout the world

Library of Congress Cataloging-in-Publication Data
Walmsley, Bonnie Brown.
    Welcome to kindergarten : a month-by-month guide to teaching and learning / Bonnie Brown Walmsley, Debra Redlo Wing.—Rev.
        p. cm.
    Includes bibliographical references.
    ISBN 0-325-00711-X (alk. paper)
    1. Kindergarten—Methods and manuals.   2. Kindergarten teachers—Handbooks, manuals, etc.
I. Wing, Debra Redlo.   II. Title.

LB1169.W265 2004
372.21'8—dc22   2004008512

Editor: Danny Miller
Production: Lynne Reed
Cover design: Catherine Hawkes, Cat & Mouse
Cover photograph: Bonnie Brown Walmsley
Typesetter: TechBooks
Manufacturing: Steve Bernier

Printed in the United States of America on acid-free paper
08 07 06 05   VP   2 3 4 5

Contents

Foreword

Each year thousands of teachers launch some five million young children on their journey through kindergarten—their first year in the big school. When the parents of today's kindergartners started school it was very likely their first regular experience in an out-of-home setting; for most youngsters today, however, the kindergarten year is one of transition from a preschool setting to the formal institution that will dominate their lives for a dozen more years.

More than forty years ago when my own children began their school careers, their kindergarten sessions lasted for little more than two hours per day. Today, more than half of the country's kindergartens offer a full-day program, and the percentage of full-day programs is likely to continue its steady increase. Furthermore, for many children for whom the kindergarten is only half-day, the rest of their day is spent in another group setting such as a child care center or family day care home.

Forty years ago any kind of formal instruction was not expected to occur until the first grade, even though some children (as in the case of one of my three) could read quite well during the kindergarten year. But today's kindergarten teachers are under increasing pressure to subject children to intense instruction in basic literacy and numeracy skills, often in ways that are now referred to as "scripted" lessons—previously referred to as "direct instruction." All over the U.S., teachers are now expected to prepare young children to meet state and national standards, and to undergo extensive testing. Their teachers are expected to produce outcomes and to achieve benchmarks, even though there is no scientific evidence that such pressures to meet performance standards actually improve young people's intellectual competence in the long run.

Long experience and recent evidence suggests that the quality of children's kindergarten experiences contributes substantially to how they come to feel about school and how they adapt to it from then onward. A recent analysis of evidence comparing more and less effective primary school teachers, their approaches to motivation, to the variety of activities they offer, and their management of their classes, supports the rich variety of suggestions offered in this book (Bohn, Roehrig, & Pressley 2004). Furthermore, a recent review of the available evidence concerning what aspects of classroom practice help young children become *engaged* in their school room life also supports the many suggestions included here by Walmsley and Wing (Fredericks, Blumenfeld, & Paris 2004). Practical suggestions of how to get these good, essential, and engaging experiences going are clearly presented for each month of the school year.

While Walmsley and Wing are clearly individuals with their own unique histories, styles, and favorite strategies, both are kindergarten teachers marked by the determination and energy required for getting every single one of their pupils off to the right start. Month by month these two able teachers take us with them on the journeys they provide for their kindergartners: from their initial introduction to life in their classrooms in August, as they gradually come to feel at home in them, through to their readiness to move on to the next set of challenges by June when they express their thanks to their teachers and say their good-byes.

All the basics are here. They are described in down-to-earth language and interesting detail beginning with the preparation period during the month of August, and including arranging the room and the materials, writing letters to the parents, as well as getting to know each child. The variety of ways to communicate with parents not only includes the usual processes and products, but even a website that grandparents can enjoy!

Walmsley and Wing share with us how they capitalize on opportunities to introduce basic academic skills, how to introduce early reading in a variety of ways, and, sprinkled throughout the rich presentation, they help us keep the principles of developmentally appropriate practice in mind while simultaneously addressing the standards required of them. They also describe a variety of useful assessment strategies and how they serve different but important purposes. Included here are many lists of recommended books on the children's level about the many topics the authors discuss.

These two teachers are certainly up front about the tension and fatigue and stresses and strains of their work, noting that they easily spend half their waking hours on their teaching and its related activities. It is easy to realize from their descriptions of their work, and the ample photographic representations of what they accomplish, how these two teachers combine personal warmth and responsiveness to each individual child with very serious attention to their learning. They are dedicated teachers who show us vividly how they gain satisfaction from the very hard work they do.

Experienced kindergarten teachers will surely find in this book some fresh ideas as well as some reassurances about their own practices; new teachers will find many useful strategies to try, as well as real inspiration to be engaged in one of the country's most important professions.

—*Lilian G. Katz, Ph.D.*
Professor Emerita
University of Illinois

References

Bohn, Catherine M., Roehrig, Alysia D., & Pressley, Michael. 2004. "The First Days of School in the Classrooms of Two More Effective and Four Less Effective Primary-Grades Teachers." *The Elementary School Journal* 104(4): 269–287.

Fredericks, Jennifer A., Blumenfeld, Phyllis C., & Paris, Alison H. 2004. "School Engagement: The Potential of the Concept, State of the Evidence." *Review of Educational Research* 74(1): 59–109.

Acknowledgments

Bonnie and Debra

It seems fitting to begin by acknowledging the members of the Kindergarten Support Group. They share our passion for this unique profession and we have learned much together over the years. First, to Abby Weber, whose boundless enthusiasm and love of teaching is contagious. She is a dear friend and valued colleague. To Harriet Fogarty, whose ability to stay the course and not lose sight of what is truly important is inspiring. Her kindness and wit are equally delightful. To Charlene Dare, Joanne Gabriele, and Nancy Sherwood. All are thoughtful and caring kindergarten teachers, and we have learned from each of them.

To Danny Miller, our editor who supported and guided us from the start and who had the courage to tell us to lose the bad jokes.

To our production editor, Lynne Reed, and copy editor, Elizabeth Tripp, for their guidance and expertise.

Thank you to Sylvia Chard for helping us expand our understanding of the project approach in our kindergarten classrooms.

Thank you to Lilian Katz. Your work has guided and inspired us throughout our careers as early childhood educators. Reading your books and articles and hearing you speak at conferences has had a profound effect on our teaching practices.

Bonnie

To the children—they are the reason I still love this profession after almost thirty years. When I'm asked to sign a book that I've written, I often write, "Never underestimate a kindergartner!" They are truly amazing little people and not a day goes by that I don't learn something from my kindergartners. I thank each and every one of them, wherever they may be.

To the parents and families at Karigon School, who are amazing. They have always been such a joy to work with. They have volunteered so generously in the classroom, read with their children, provided nutritious snacks, saved their "good junk" for our projects, and entrusted me with their children as they have begun their education.

To Debra Wing, who has been a wonderful colleague over the years, and more recently a diligent collaborator as we put in some long hours to complete this book.

To my principal, Doug Johnson, and more recently, Greg Wing, and many colleagues at Karigon School for their support and encouragement.

To Faith Higgins for being a real team player as she supported the special needs students in my class and laughed at my kindergarten humor.

To my friends Kathy Geary, Mary MacDonald, Cindy Spence, and Susan Towne, who helped me keep a balance and provided me with some social life and a chance to discuss something other than kindergarten.

To my mother, Renita Brown, who taught all four of her children to be independent and encouraged us to follow our dreams.

To my brother, Marc Brown, and sisters, Colleen Quadri and Kim Brown, who provided support and levity via email. No danger of taking myself too seriously with them around!

To my son, Jonathan, who has taught me to be a more accepting and compassionate teacher. I have learned that each child is truly unique.

To my daughter, Katharine, who read the first draft and provided valuable advice through the eyes of a graduate student in education. As always, her insights were thoughtful, clear, and wise beyond her years. Our profession needs many more like her.

And last but not least, to my husband, Sean. We coauthored my four previous books and I could have never done them without him. This time he set me free, which was both liberating and a bit frightening. Thanks for all the technical and moral support and the time and freedom to get it done.

Debra

My first thank-you is to my dear colleague and friend Bonnie, who suggested we work together to create a book for kindergarten teachers. It was a pleasure to work with Bonnie. We always found the humor and laughed a lot at ourselves.

I wish to thank Nancy Andress, our assistant superintendent for curriculum and instruction, for her ability to nurture dreams and help turn them into practice. Her unwavering support is courageous and beyond measure.

I wish to thank my inspiring colleagues at Westmere. It would be hard to find a more committed, creative, or outstanding group of teachers. Walking through the hall each day, talking with my colleagues, and seeing their classrooms have been gifts to me. In particular, I wish to thank Dorine Phelan and Robert Whiteman for partnering with me in so many ways and especially in our project approach to curriculum. Sharing that journey with them moved me more deeply in my knowledge and performance as a teacher.

I am also so grateful for how much we have laughed together at school and on trips and for our planning and presenting together. We always seem to be creating higher levels of learning for each other. And a special thank-you to Ann Vaughn and Lisa O'Brien for their unwavering support and encouragement.

I wish to thank my principal, Debbie Drumm, for her enthusiastic support and great confidence in me as a kindergarten teacher. I also want to thank Debbie for possessing abundant early childhood knowledge and demonstrating a deep commitment to creating an outstanding school.

For all the parents who have expressed warm wishes for success with my book, I want to say a sincere thank-you for your unequivocal support. Most of all, I want to express how fortunate I have been to work with you and your beautiful children.

I wish to thank two area professional organizations. The first is the Capital District Association for the Education of Young Children and, in particular, Marilyn Cohen, for her insightful and creative leadership. Her support and collaboration in bringing remarkable programs to the area for early childhood teachers and her willingness to partner with diverse educational groups have been exceptional. The second thank-you is for the Greater Capital Region Teacher Center, which helped spearhead many high-quality workshops and seminars and, in particular, a sincere thank-you to Ellen Sullivan for her innovative ideas and special support for kindergarten teachers and programs.

I want to express my love for my two beautiful children, Josh and Laura. I want to thank them for their patience and understanding with a mom who was writing a book. They now have an indelible imprint of their mom sitting at the computer. Thank you for understanding some hasty and self-made dinners. I have learned so much about being a better teacher through having you. I am forever grateful.

Last are my parents, who canopied me with much love and support throughout my life. My dad is no longer physically present, but his lessons shared throughout my growing up remain with me. His most powerful proverb was "A journey of a thousand miles begins with the first step." My dad gave me the power to set a course and follow my goals. I have loved my course and can think of no greater joy than to be with children each day.

Introductions: Starting the Journey

Bonnie's

When Debra and I started this book, we struggled a bit as to how we could write using a single voice and yet retain our individuality. We share a philosophy and many practices in our kindergartens, but we are also two individuals with different backgrounds, education, and teaching experiences. We feel those individual differences help create a richer and more thoughtful book. So before we join together and become one voice, we'd like to share how we have each arrived at the place where this journey begins.

I am the second of four children: an older brother, Marc, and two younger sisters, Colleen and Kim. We grew up just outside of Erie, Pennsylvania, in Millcreek. My father worked for the railroad and my mother was a housewife. We caught salamanders in the creek, swung from grapevines, played kickball, swam in the lake, and rode our bikes everywhere.

I have wonderful memories of my Grandma Thora telling us bedtime stories that she would make up as she went along. She often rubbed our backs as she sent us off to sleep with one of her tales. It was so soothing to hear the sound of her voice and the descriptive language as she spun a story for us. We would beg for spooky stories because she would take out her false teeth and make funny faces.

My first experience with formal education was kindergarten. In the '50s many public schools did not have kindergartens, and my parents decided I would attend the local private Catholic kindergarten. It was housed in a lovely old Tudor-style building shaded by big maple trees. I was very shy as a young child and often hid behind my grandmother's skirt when we went places. When I began kindergarten I remember being very excited but also very apprehensive. I arrived well prepared and ready for business with a black three-ring binder filled with notebook paper that I had borrowed from my father. I was not in the door more than a few minutes when a nun snatched my notebook and informed me that I would not be needing it. That made an indelible impression on me. From that moment on, I did not want to be there. Oh, I enjoyed the music and using the rhythm sticks and I remember playing outdoors on the slide, but that's all I remember. Luckily, I came down with rheumatic fever by November and was kept home and exiled to the sofa for several months and happily never returned to kindergarten. The doctor visited regularly (talk about the good old days!) and I had plenty of visitors bearing books, puzzles, and brownies. And when nobody was around, I would jump up and down on the sofa.

The following September I began first grade at Lakewood Elementary, a two-story brick building with those very tall windows, black slate chalkboards, built-in oak cupboards, and coat hooks along the back of each classroom with a picture of George Washington hanging above them. Mrs. Crandall was a tall, ageless, even-tempered, stern but kind woman. I remember Dick, Jane, Sally, Spot, and Puff and sitting in rows and meeting in reading groups in the back of the classroom. And I remember the thrill of going upstairs to the school library, which consisted of one narrow room with a long wooden table in the middle and shelves of books from top to bottom on either side. All things considered, my early education improved at Lakewood.

This may be a good time to mention that my brother is Marc Brown, author and illustrator of the Arthur books. The characters and many of the places in the Arthur books are based on people and places in our childhood. Arthur also attends Lakewood School and hangs out after school at the Sugar Bowl, just like we did. Like Arthur, my principal was Mr. Haney and I had a good friend named Muffy. And I am the inspiration for Francine, the charming, tomboy monkey friend of Arthur's. I guess I should have been nicer to Marc when we were kids! D. W. is a combination of all three of Marc's younger sisters (plenty of material there). And Mr. Ratburn is based on one of our teachers, who shall remain nameless.

I always loved sports and was accomplished at most of them. In the '60s there weren't many girls athletic teams in school, so I spent lots of time playing with the boys, teaching swimming lessons, and doing gymnastics. During high school I competed in gymnastics, was a good student, went to the football games and the prom. When it was time to choose a college, I picked the one with the best women's gymnastics team I could find (not a strategy I would recommend) and headed to Kent State University. After a stint as a physical education major and a French major (can't imagine what I was thinking on that one), I landed in the early childhood education program. This turned out to be a huge stroke of luck for me. I was excited by the coursework and ecstatic with student teaching. I had found my niche.

After graduation I headed to Boston because my college boyfriend had gone there to practice architecture (another of my well-thought-out plans). When I got to Boston I moved in with my brother, Marc, and his wife and began looking for a teaching job. Unfortunately, a bachelor's degree in education was not all that marketable in Boston in the mid-'70s. The waitresses had master's degrees. But eventually I landed a job teaching in Headstart in Roxbury. When I began teaching, I was hopeless, and by the time I left two years later, I had learned so much and was doing a respectable job. Since I was riding a bike, sharing an apartment with four other women, and eating tuna sandwiches or granola for dinner most nights, I decided it might be a good idea to get a master's degree.

So I got myself a big fat loan and headed across the river to Harvard Graduate School of Education. I decided to get a degree in reading and proceeded to work like I'd never worked before in school. I was very fortunate to study with Carol Chomsky, Jeanne Chall, Helen Popp, and Courtney Cazden. The time I spent at Harvard has had an enormous impact on the way I teach early literacy and started me on a road that has made me a more thoughtful and reflective teacher. So I left Harvard with a master's degree in reading and a husband (all right, I wasn't studying all the time!) and headed to upstate New York, where my husband had taken a job in the reading department at the University at Albany and I had a job teaching first grade in the school district where I still teach today. I had hoped to get a job teaching first grade, so I was a very happy person.

Throughout my career I have taught first grade and second grade and have been teaching kindergarten for the past eighteen years. My husband, Sean, and I have had countless discussions, debates, and—yes!—even some disagreements about issues in education. I have learned from all of these experiences. We have raised two bright and creative children from whom I have learned both the strengths and the weaknesses of public education. I have been very fortunate to work in a supportive district with countless cooperative, caring, and loving families. But I have learned the most from the children. It is the children that make this job exciting, exhausting, and one of the most satisfying and rewarding careers I can imagine.

About ten years ago I attended a workshop for kindergarten teachers sponsored by our local Capital Region Teacher Center. After the series of workshops were completed, a group of us decided it might be helpful to continue meeting. We have been meeting for the past eleven years now in each other's homes, classrooms, summer cottages, bookstores, and restaurants. We have attended conferences, presented at conferences, and visited schools and museums together. We have squashed five in a hotel room (hey, hotels are expensive in New York City!), helped one member through her fear of flying, finished a few bottles of wine together, celebrated birthdays, and been there for each other as our children became adolescents, got their driver's licenses, and headed to college. We've had many good times and a few sad times, but through it all we have learned so much from each other about kindergarten.

Sadly, one of our group has died after a courageous battle with breast cancer, two have retired, and a few have changed grade levels, but there is still a group of us that meets regularly to share ideas, books, experiences, opinions, and lots of laughs. This is where I am now and this is where we begin our journey through a year in kindergarten.

Debra's

My journey to become a teacher began when I was a young girl growing up in New York City. I am part of the baby boom generation. For me this meant that I had fifty-two children in my first-grade class. During this time if you got sick and stayed home, you lost your desk and were rotated to sit on the long ledge at the back of the class. During my childhood, kids got every childhood disease—mumps, chicken pox, measles, and so on—so it was not uncommon to be out a good deal. After a weeklong bout with the mumps, I came back to school and had to sit with my books and coat on the back ledge. The teacher seemed a mile away, and I tried with all my might to sit still and pass the time as painlessly as possible. For me that meant daydreaming, looking out the window, anything to help endure the long, uncomfortable day. The only way you could get a seat back again was to wait for someone else in the class to get sick and then rotate into his seat. Let's just say this was an educational time of unenlightenment and there was a shortage of classroom space!

I did not learn to read at all this first school year, but I was a very happy-go-lucky kid, so I probably didn't even know I was supposed to be learning to read. Like most parents in those days, my parents had complete faith in the school system, so they thought I was where I was supposed to be.

Second grade brought another unfortunate school experience. I had Mrs. Hamberger. My mother had Mrs. Hamberger when she was in second grade! Mrs. Hamberger decided to retire in October of that school year. I was still in a very large class, and from October to June (the end of the school year), we had substitute teachers for a week or two on and off. Other children did learn to read, but I did not.

My parents bought a new home in Brooklyn that summer and we moved in for the start of school in September. This was a spanking-new school and not at all overcrowded compared with what I had experienced in the old neighborhood. We had an average class size of about thirty-five. My records had not yet arrived at the new school, but my sister's had. My older sister was very smart and she did learn to read! So they assumed I was very smart like her and they placed both of us in the "1" class, as in 3-1 for me and 5-1 for Fern. In those days kids were grouped homogeneously. Educators at this time believed it was wise to group kids of like ability together. I realize how far we have come in our thinking and our practices. It is abundantly evident to me as a teacher today how much children learn from each other. It seems like it was the dark ages when I went to school. And I grew up in New York City!

I began third grade barely knowing my letters, knowing not a blessed sound, and certainly having no clue how to read. If I were in my current teaching district,

I would probably have been tested up and down for some type of learning disability. In some ways so many kids in the class saved me because no one really noticed my deficits or me and I was not made to feel any different than all my friends. But this was about to change.

I managed to escape to the girls room the first week of third grade in my new school when the teacher was doing round-robin reading. I was able to time it just right to be passed over at my turn. But after a week the teacher must have noticed she had not heard from me and came back to me when I returned to my seat. When she called my name I can still remember my shame and embarrassment. I broke out into a cold sweat and I wanted to fall beneath my desk. I don't know who was more horrified, my teacher or I.

The next day when I came to school I was asked to gather all my belongings and sit in a chair in the hall. I noticed other children sitting in chairs outside their classroom doors and I wondered what this was all about. In some ways I was secretly relieved because I thought, "Good, I won't have to do the round-robin reading this morning." When another boy was placed in the hall close by I whispered across to him, "Hi, do you know why we are out here?"

He answered, "Yeah we're getting placed in a new class. It's for all the dummies." Although I should have been mortified, I was feeling more confused. In time we were placed in a new room, and to our delight, a young teacher with a kind voice and warm demeanor greeted us. At the end of the day I had a letter to take home to my parents explaining the change and my new class.

My parents were wonderful people and I heard them talking that evening. They just didn't realize I had been so behind because I was a happy, active, and friendly kid. They worked up a plan that was later to become my foundation for choosing a teaching career. This plan was possible because my dad worked evenings and he was home when I returned from school each day.

My dad did some investigating and came up with a plan to teach me to read. He got a set of tapes for the tape recorder that would guide the lessons, and he would fill in from there. I was to work with him directly after school for two hours, Monday through Friday. My dad was very patient with me. I stumbled quite a bit in the first few months and I know there were times he was amazed that I was still forgetting some basic words and sounds. My dad still seemed so happy to see me after school. I sure was tying up two hours of his time each day. He made the lessons like a game and kept it fast-paced and it was not as painful as I had thought it would be. I missed riding my bike and playing with friends after school, but I did need to learn to read. It was a long fall, winter, and spring, but at last I was a reader.

At the end of my elementary school years, in the sixth grade, I had to take a test for junior high school placement. I did very well and qualified to have a second language class for seventh, eighth, and ninth grade.

A gift other than learning to read that has stayed with me all my life is the capacity to work hard on things and to plug away. My dad showed me that just about any job could be accomplished with teamwork and commitment and by beginning each journey with the first step.

At the end of high school I had some college choices as long as they were in New York City! My first choice was Brooklyn College and I got in. The college had a newly organized teacher education program. Many of the college teachers and professors were forward thinking and believed in the principles of John Dewey, Maria Montessori, Jean Piaget, Erik Erikson, and Sylvia Ashton-Warner. In fact, the program felt so rigorous that many of us undergraduates talked about leaving the major for something else. This was especially true during the two student teaching experiences. I honestly did not know how teachers did it. I was completely spent at the end of the teaching day and I would go home and collapse. I felt discouraged and wondered if you work your whole teaching career this way. Sometimes the answer to that thought is yes. But of course the beauty of teaching for a while is that you do get more efficient, you learn to pace yourself, and most importantly, you learn to enjoy the children and get energy from their enthusiasm and love.

When I graduated from college, teaching jobs were very hard to find. In fact, the New York City licensing exam was not given that year because there were so many applicants on the waiting list. But there is always a silver lining and because I did not land a steady position right away, I worked in a wide variety of settings (as a fill-in substitute) that taught me varying philosophies and methods and showed me a diverse range of classroom environments. I worked in a day care center at Co-Op City in the Bronx, a Montessori school in Brooklyn, and a private school on Park Avenue in New York City. In every school the children responded to warmth, kindness, and teaching with enthusiasm, respect, and caring.

During these first jobs I was extremely fortunate to hear about a special school for teacher training. It had a funny name: Bank Street College of Education. After learning more about the college, I applied, and to my happiness, they accepted me. Many of my college teachers wrote the books we were assigned in our education courses. Models from and learning at Bank Street remain with me today.

I moved to upstate New York when I was twenty-five. I landed a job teaching second grade at a private prep school for boys. Because I had a great deal of academic freedom and was allowed to be as creative as I could or wanted to be, I loved my teaching years there.

During this time I had my daughter, Laura, and my son, Joshua. I always thought I was an empathetic teacher and that I was sensitive to parents, but having my own children opened my heart much wider, and my ability to empathize with the feelings of my families grew greatly. I better understood exhaustion, frustration, and how vulnerable a parent feels when all is not going well with a child's learning or development. As always I would share and ask parents to join in a partnership if there were behaviors or academic concerns that needed addressing, but if that partnership could not happen for whatever reason(s), I now acted on the principle that I would not worry or wait for the parent's contribution but instead would do all that was possible in my classroom and the school setting. I now knew and felt the tremendous responsibility of the parenting job. I also knew that for some parents this put them over the edge because they were already stretched pretty thin.

One public school district in my area was like a beacon atop a lighthouse. When I and other teachers wanted to know some of the newest ideas and how they were being implemented, we pointed in the same direction, Guilderland Schools. I went to observe how the district's teachers were using a readers and writers workshop. For its teachers' professional development in this area, the district had flown in Lucy Calkins and colleagues from the Columbia Teachers College Writing Project to train and model lessons monthly. Guilderland did away with reading series and workbooks long before this practice became mainstream. Every teacher in the Guilderland district was trained in readers and writers workshop and had regular follow-up training and support for two years.

Although I loved my current teaching position, I was ready for a new professional experience and some challenges, so when a parent informed me of an opening in the Guilderland district, I applied. I went on a series of interviews and to my amazement and delight, I was offered a position. When I first joined the district, I felt woefully inadequate because people who had been immersed in an exceptional educational culture surrounded me. With support, outstanding working conditions (such as a full-time teaching assistant in kindergarten), long hours, and what felt like more professional development than my master's program, I began to feel confident and capable.

Our local teacher center knew that kindergarten teachers are a unique group. The center thought kindergarten teachers would want to meet for professional camaraderie and sharing of ideas. We kindergarten teachers began to meet about ten years ago. A core of us developed such a fondness and respect for each other that we never stopped meeting. In fact, we grew closer by attending workshops together and very soon thereafter presenting workshops together. We flew together to attend conferences and to hear respected leaders in our field. We studied together as we learned new approaches, most notably writers workshop for kindergartners and the project approach.

Many of us in the Kindergarten Support Group have shared locally and nationally. Bonnie and I have presented, shared, discussed, and debated many a topic pertaining to all aspects of kindergarten. This book grew out of a trip we took to collect free contact paper at a local factory. While driving there, we talked about Bonnie's success with her books and thought perhaps there was a need for a new book that shared our current ideas and practices. At the inception it sounded like a terrific idea. Bonnie was experienced and I knew this would be an exciting and rewarding collaboration. I was a bit mystified when she held her enthusiasm in check. Two years later and after many long work sessions, together and separately, I know why! But writing together has been another wonderful journey.

August

Starting Again

In August we return to our classrooms to set up for a new year and new challenges. We set up and organize our classrooms as well as write welcome letters and create options for children and parents to visit the classroom before school begins. August is also a time to do something for ourselves. We are avid gardeners, love swimming and tennis, reading and traveling. August is the time we relax and recharge so we can meet the demands of another kindergarten year. But when late August arrives, we are back in our classrooms, cleaning, organizing, repainting, and setting up. We know the next few months will be challenging and also very rewarding.

Welcome to Kindergarten Letter

An important August job is to send a letter to our incoming parents and kindergartners. Debra's letter is more extensive and Bonnie's is brief because she will be meeting with parents and children in small groups during the first three days of school. We include a short introduction to acquaint the parents with the kindergarten program, our philosophy, and learning goals. We also describe some of the routines and established practices in the kindergarten program. The following are things we have addressed over the years:

Communication: We let parents know we will be sending home a weekly or biweekly newsletter, each child will need a pocket folder to carry papers to and from school, when parent-teacher conferences will be, and how parents can contact us when they have a question or concern. We do give parents our home phone numbers and email addresses and encourage them to send a note to school with their child for things that are not urgent.

Transportation: We let the parents know how to notify us if their child will be riding home on a different bus or will be picked up at dismissal or early for an appointment.

Snack: In Bonnie's class the parents take turns sending in the snack for the entire class. Each family has a turn roughly once a month. Bonnie has had great success asking for fruits and/or vegetables for the daily snack. Grapes, carrots, apples, bananas, pineapple chunks, raisins, and other dried fruits are favorites. Clementines are also good because they are not too large and are easy to peel. In Debra's class the parents are guided with a list of suggested snacks. Candy, soda, and other nonnutritious foods are not acceptable. Children who have cheese and crackers or yogurt and fruit may feel cheated if they see a classmate eating chips or candy. We encourage the use of reusable containers for packing snack items. We are not just filling their tummies but teaching them about nutrition and encouraging them to try new things they may not sample at home. We are also teaching about the environment in a way that kindergartners can make a contribution.

Birthdays: We explain how we celebrate in school. We prefer to keep birthdays simple and ask parents to send treats that are tasty yet not junk food. Oatmeal cookies, pumpkin muffins, blueberry muffins, and rice crispy treats are a few we suggest. Of course we need to be well aware of allergies and when we have a severe allergy in the classroom, we limit choices further.

Outdoor Play: We suggest children wear appropriate clothing, especially sturdy and comfortable footwear.

Supplies: We ask parents for some supplies but try to be sensitive to how much we ask parents to provide. When parents have a few children in school, it all adds up.

We end our summer letter to the parents by telling them how much we look forward to working with them and their child in the coming year. We want to be welcoming and reassuring because some families are sending their first child to the large elementary school and may be apprehensive.

Debra also sends a note to each child. She makes this light and upbeat. She tells the child a few things she will be learning and may mention a field trip that will happen in September. Sometimes she encloses a piece of drawing paper for the child to draw a picture. Parents can drop the picture off at school or the child can bring it in on the first day. Debra makes an opening bulletin board with these pictures and names.

We believe that taking a little time in August to prepare and send a welcoming letter sets a positive tone with the parents and fosters feelings of trust and warmth.

Getting Ready

Barn Raising

Debra does a "barn raising" at the end of each summer. A classroom barn raising is a way to accomplish many jobs around the classroom before the opening of school. She announces this event to her parents in her Welcome to Kindergarten letter. It works best if it is in the evening and for adults only. Following are some possible jobs parents can do:

- paint doors, trim, and play equipment
- cover new and worn paperback books with clear contact paper
- replace bulletin board paper to prepare for displaying children's work
- clean shelves for books, blocks, and paper
- organize art paper
- stamp all class books with identifying stamp
- set up class aquarium

Debra provides drinks, a light snack, and name tags. She records the names of those who participate and follows up with thank-you notes. In addition to her classroom getting much cleaner and more organized, she gets to meet some of her incoming parents. She gets to spend time with the parents who often become some of the most hardworking and supportive parents in the coming school year. The atmosphere is informal and friendly and parents who are anxious get a chance to meet the teacher.

The Giving Tree

The Giving Tree is a way to let parents know what is needed to help supply the classroom for the year. If we keep requests for each child's supplies to a minimum, most parents are willing to donate an item or two on the Giving Tree. It is also optional so parents don't feel pressured to purchase items they can't afford. Bonnie puts her Giving Tree up when the parents and children come to school for the first three days of school. Debra has hers up for her barn raising and Open House night. This way all parents have an opportunity to contribute.

Supplies requested on the tree may include tissues, zip-top bags, film, photo developing, birdseed, drinking cups, clay, and any other supply items that are not provided by the school.

Meet the Teacher Book

We have each made a book to introduce ourselves to our families. The books are only about ten pages long, with photos of our families, homes, gardens, and things

Figure 1–1. The Giving Tree

that help the children get to know us. We laminated the books and we put them in our class libraries at the start of school.

Setting Up the Classroom

During August we reflect on the previous years and inevitably do some rearranging. Through many years of trial and error, we know that it works best to keep the noisier activities at one end of the classroom. Quieter areas like a cozy book nook or a writing center are in another corner and an art area is near a sink and preferably on uncarpeted floor. We also make space for a large meeting area with enough room to dance.

Figure 1–2. Block organization

Building

Building toys and dramatic play tend to be noisy activities. For that reason we have them on a carpeted area at one end of the classroom. We have the blocks organized on shelves where they can be stored while not in use and we stack the large hollow blocks in this area as well. We also store other building toys such as vehicles, signs, Lego toys, marble runs, duplo toys, tabletop blocks, and bristle blocks on a shelf nearby. There is a chalkboard where children can represent their block structures with drawings. There is also a large wooden dollhouse with furniture and people that is easily accessible to the children.

Dramatic Play

The dramatic play area begins the year as a housekeeping center. It has a stove, sink, refrigerator, table, cupboard, doll bed, high chair, dress-up clothes, dishes, food, telephones, and so on. We think it is important to have this area well equipped so rich and involved dramatic play will occur. Cleanup is easier if there is a place for everything. We also have a place to store the puppets nearby. As different themes and projects develop, it is worthwhile to change the dramatic play area to enhance the theme or project; for example, we have turned the area into a bakery, doctor's office, farm stand, drive-up bank, and fairy tale theater (see p. 14).

Figure 1–3. Housekeeping cottage

Figure 1–4. Dramatic play area as a fairy tale theater

Figure 1–5. Meeting area

Meeting Area

At the opposite end of the room we have another carpeted space. This is where we meet to start the day. We have made sure it is large enough for all of us to sit on the floor in our circle and also for Music and Movement. We have found that putting a round rug on top of the carpet helps the children easily form a circle. We also have a large easel at one end near the calendar. We use the easel for the daily message and reading big books.

Library

Our library is not limited to one specific area. Surrounding our meeting area are countertops, tables, and shelves where we display theme-related materials. We place books as well as other items children have brought to share on these surfaces in attractive displays. Additional books related to the theme are on a bookstand near the theme center. We also have a stand for big books, one to display books written by the author or illustrator we are highlighting, and one to be

Figure 1–6. Classroom library

changed as needed. Some beanbag chairs and cushions make it comfy and very inviting to snuggle up with a favorite book. We don't keep all the books in this library area. Near the math area we have a rubber dishpan full of counting books and number books. When the science museum is set up, we place books related to the exhibits in that area. We group books in many ways and display them throughout the year. Rhyming books, silly books, books the children have written, books the children can read, nonfiction books, and alphabet books are some of the ways we might organize books. If we change books regularly and highlight them in different ways, children will be drawn to them and read more. Books that are left in boxes for the entire year for children to flip through are not nearly so enticing. We have taken a lesson from the retail business and arrange books so children are eager to read them.

Art Area

In the middle of the classroom we have a large uncarpeted area that we use for art projects, snack time, and as a writing area. The art area is near a sink, a countertop, some shelves, and a cupboard with doors that store many art materials. Near the easels there is a table for art projects and tucked nearby on low hooks are multiple smocks for art projects or water play. When setting up the art area, these are some materials we have found most helpful: a variety of sizes and colors of paper, tempera paints, watercolors, various-sized paintbrushes, crayons, markers, scissors, glue, chalk, craypas, clay (plasticine), play dough, pencils, and fine-tip pens for sketching. For specific projects, we add various recycled materials or items purchased from craft stores or catalogs. There is so much available. The possibilities are endless.

Many items needed for art projects can also be obtained free of charge from various businesses and shops. For example, framing shops are usually happy to donate scraps of matte board. We have a company near us that donates all kinds of contact paper to teachers. Woodworkers often donate scraps of wood. We are not shy about asking anymore because we have found people to be very generous. If we give the donor a receipt, he can often use it for tax purposes. Parents are also a great resource. Many parents work in places where they can obtain donations. If we have a parent who works at a paper company, that can be a gold mine!

Recycled items are wonderful for art projects. We make a list at the beginning of the year and ask parents to start saving. Be sure to emphasize the items must be clean or it may become a science experiment! Some items we have found useful are buttons, beads, corks, yarn, shells, bottle caps, fabric scraps, marker lids, milk lids, juice lids (any lids!), yogurt containers, spools, packaging materials, toilet paper tubes, acorns, film canisters, wood scraps, pasta, feathers, wrapping paper, ribbons, and anything else that can be used for collages, sculptures, or projects. We have a large box in the classroom labeled "Beautiful Junk" where children can deposit the materials as they bring them to school. Later we can sort the items and place them in various containers.

For the smaller items, we think clear plastic containers work best because teachers and children can see the contents. A book that has inspired us to use recycled materials in new and exciting ways is *Beautiful Stuff!* by Cathy Weisman Topal and Lella Gandini (1999). This book was inspired by the work in Reggio Emilia, Italy.

Writing Area

At the writing center we have tables and chairs to seat about ten children. This is a popular area because the children love to draw and write. We also have shelves that are clearly labeled with pictures and words where we store markers, crayons, pencils, glue, tape, stencils, rubber stamps and stamp pads, colored pencils, and a variety of paper. After some additional training in writers workshop

Figure 1–7. Writing area

this past summer, we are now putting out an assortment of prepared blank books that we have made by stapling three to ten pieces of paper together. When the children put their own books together, we encourage careful paper choices and keep a recycling bin handy. In this area we display a large chart showing correct letter formation and small individual charts the children can bring to the tables. We have tabletop easels to display charts and posters relating to the theme that help expand vocabulary and language.

Math Area

We have several shelves on which to store all the math manipulatives. There are balances, number puzzles, games, pattern blocks, learning links, Unifix cubes, pegs and peg boards, dominoes, sorting trays, and more. We provide a variety of counters; some we have purchased and many we have collected. Shells, acorns, buttons, keys, bottle caps, and old marker tops are just some of the items we have collected. We try to be creative and use items that relate to our themes when possible.

Figure 1–8. Writing area supplies

Figure 1–9. Math area

We begin in the fall by putting about six or seven items out on the shelves and after the children have had time to explore those, we add additional materials. There is a table and rug nearby where children can use these manipulatives. We display colorful number cards with numerals and objects for the numbers one to twenty and several number books and counting books here as well.

Teacher Area

In one corner of the classroom we have a teacher's desk, computer, shelves, and filing cabinets. We frequently have notes from parents and other private papers, and it's best to have our things off to one side. The computer in our kindergarten classroom is mostly used by the teacher and an aide to create newsletters and maintain the class website. It can be a source of information for the teacher and the children for projects and themes. Sometimes the children use the computer for learning from a CD-ROM such as *Chicka Chicka Boom Boom* or art programs like Kid Pix. But mainly we want the children to have hands-on experiences that engage all of their senses and encourage social interaction. The children will have many years ahead for computer work but very few for rich experiences with sensory materials that touch and shape their foundation.

The way we arrange our classrooms becomes the basis for all we do with the children throughout the year. This allows our children to work, play, and make choices within a structure that guides them toward purposeful and developmentally appropriate experiences. This is why we are willing to forgo time in our gardens or reading one last book and return to our stuffy classrooms to reflect, make new choices, and lug furniture. Our sore muscles will subside, but the improved classroom organization will last all year.

Screening

There are many different ways to screen children before they enter kindergarten. There are a number of published screening devices and many schools create their own. Whatever screening is used, we believe it should be done for the right reasons. Screening should be used to gain information about the children and to prepare for their arrival at kindergarten. Screening should not be used to exclude children or postpone their entrance to kindergarten.

Many districts administer a screening in the spring before children enter kindergarten. The children are typically evaluated by an adult they don't know and often in a setting that is unfamiliar. Screeners may not get an accurate picture of a child's social, emotional, or cognitive abilities in this brief encounter.

These screenings can occur as much as six months prior to entering kindergarten. At this age a child can develop dramatically over a six-month period. A screening should be only one piece of information used to make a decision about a child's kindergarten experience.

If this type of screening revealed a child had speech or language delays, it would be appropriate to recommend further testing and provide services if needed. On the other hand, if a child with these delays was identified and screeners concluded that this child should simply be withheld from school an additional year, it would not be a good use of screening. These screenings are expensive and time-consuming and often take teachers and support staff away from their current students. Consider the benefits and alternatives carefully before proceeding with a screening.

In Bonnie's district, the schools use an informal screening designed by kindergarten teachers with input from specialists in teaching gifted children and children with handicapping conditions. It is administered during the first three days of school. So, while the older children in grades 1 through 5 start school, kindergartners come to school in groups of four or five with their parents to meet their new teacher, get to know some of their classmates, and become familiar with the school and their classroom. There are rarely any separation problems because the parents remain in the classroom. The kindergartners begin school the week after the rest of the children do. Because the older students are settled in, the focus can now be on getting kindergartners to and from school safely and happily.

During these meetings, Bonnie shares a wordless picture book with the children, asks them each to draw a picture and write their name, watches them play with other children, and teaches them a dance. While the children are playing and drawing, Bonnie talks to individual children and speaks with the parents. These meetings allow her to gather some basic information about each child's development. It also allows the parents to share information that they might not be comfortable sharing in a large-group setting. Getting to know the children and their parents in a more informal setting puts everyone at ease and is a wonderful way to start the year. In a large school district this creates a warmer feeling between the parents, children, and teacher. An additional benefit is that the children become familiar with the classroom and some of their classmates before the first day. After the children and parents leave, Bonnie has thirty minutes to make some notes and prepare for the next group. There are four groups in a day.

This procedure has been used for many years and it has been much more helpful than the published screening device previously used. This information is also used to meet a state mandate to screen for potentially gifted and potentially handicapped students. A screening is the first step in an evaluation process. We talk more about evaluation and assessment in the October chapter.

Summary

The month of August helps us realize how fortunate we are in the teaching profession to have a true beginning to our work each year. This beginning allows us to reflect, change, and realize our hopes for the coming year.

Since the classroom layout and environment have a powerful impact on all we do for the year ahead, we commit to setting up the most inviting, engaging, and instructive environment we can.

Parents have been their children's first teachers; therefore, we communicate with them prior to beginning the year. That is why we send a welcoming and informative letter home. We also want to open the door wide for two-way communication at the start of the school year.

We hope we have communicated our fervent beliefs about the use of screening in kindergarten. It should always be inclusive and used to inform. Screening is a way to begin learning about the children that we will guide and teach and care deeply about in the coming school year.

September

Ready, Set, Go

When our children enter kindergarten on the first day of school, we want to make them feel welcome. We strive to create an environment that is cheerful, safe, and a comfortable place to learn. We have worked hard on setting up the classroom before the children arrive on the first day.

By putting that extra time into organizing the classroom and planning the first weeks carefully, we are able to devote all our energy to the children when they arrive. And each year it takes all the energy we can muster to get the year off to a good start. In preparation for the first day, we write each child's name in a number of places. This lets them know they are expected and have a special place in our class. As we write these names now and place them in cubbies, on job charts, and on attendance cards, they are simply names. Very soon they will be much more than names on some cards.

On the first day we set up some centers that are open-ended and high interest; blocks, paints, and play dough are good choices. We provide name tags so we can address each child by name and learn their names quickly. We greet each child with a smile, hoping they will feel this is a friendly and inviting environment. A calm, reassuring, and cheerful approach sets the tone and the children sense we are experienced and caring teachers. We want the children to know this will be a great year and they will have a wonderful time in kindergarten, meeting new friends and playing and learning each day.

Daily Routines

We feel it is critical to establish well-thought-out routines that provide a balanced day for young children. Daily routines will vary depending on the length of the kindergarten day. We have outlined what a full- and a half-day kindergarten might look like in the following sections. Although the length of the day might vary from school to school, the basic routines can be the same. Daily routines are important in kindergarten. They provide structure and predictability to the day, and all children need that. The schedules that follow include routines that we have found beneficial. Many districts still have two half-day kindergartens and consequently teachers have a morning and an afternoon session each day. The first schedule is based on a half-day kindergarten and the second outlines a full day. The times are approximate. Although routine is important, we allow for flexibility in our daily schedules. Our daily routines and schedules have been developed through many years of teaching and are based on the work of educators such as Dewey, Vygotsky, Paley, Cambourne, Clay, Strickland, Katz, and Chard.

Full-Day Kindergarten Schedule

Following is a schedule for a six-hour session.

8:00   Coming-in Activities
8:30   Morning Announcements
8:35   Cleanup
8:40   Morning Meeting (meet in a circle on the rug)

- can start with a rain stick or other instrument to set the tone
- open meeting with a song or greeting or both
- share items related to theme
- write and read a morning message
- count and record days of school
- calendar
- share parent comments about traveling class-made books
- share items in mystery bag
- read journal of class mascot or bear
- create interactive charts such as "How many letters are in your name?"
- do a whole-group activity such as a math activity or phonemic awareness activity

We would not recommend doing all of these activities each day. We try to move it right along and be sensitive to the children's attention spans.

9:00   Music and Movement: dancing, singing, instruments
9:15   Read-Aloud: some possibilities are

- theme-related fiction or nonfiction
- big books for shared reading

- poetry
- story discussions, extensions, or dramatizations

9:30 Center Time/Choice Time (Snack is put out at this time and children can either go to the snack table as a scheduled activity or at their leisure.)

11:00 Lunch and Outside Play

12:00 Relax and Read

12:25 Writers Workshop, Science Activity or Small-Group Work (targeting children at risk and those needing an additional challenge)

1:00 Special Area Classes: art, music, computer, physical education, library (Offerings and length of these classes will vary from school to school.)

1:30 Choice Time: children choose puzzles, clay, drawing, painting, water table, etc.

2:00 Class Meeting

- read aloud (We recommend a shorter work of fiction for the end of the day that relates to a current theme.)
- share children's art or writing
- draw closure to the day

2:15 Pack Up and Dismissal

Half-Day Kindergarten Schedule

Following is a schedule for a two-hour-and-forty-five-minute session. (We elaborate on these components and routines in the full-day schedule and later in this chapter.)

7:55 Coming-in Time

8:10 Morning Meeting (see full-day schedule for components of morning meeting)

8:30 Music and Movement

8:45 Read-Aloud

9:00 Center Time/Choice Time

10:00 Cleanup

10:10 Relax and Read or Outside Play

10:30 Closing

10:40 Dismissal

When teaching two half-days, teachers often have one hour between sessions for lunch and a break. At other grade levels or in a full-day kindergarten, teachers receive their break when students attend art, music, or physical education.

In the fall of 1998, 55 percent of children attending kindergarten in the United States were attending full-day programs and 45 percent were in half-day programs. Although the research indicates other factors contribute to children's success in kindergarten, it does appear that a full-day kindergarten is beneficial academically and socially to many children, especially those at risk. Researchers also warn that it is important to remember that what children are doing during the kindergarten day is more important than the length of the day. Gullo (1990) and Olsen and Zigler (1989) warn educators and parents to resist the pressure to include more didactic academic instruction. They contend that this type of instruction is inappropriate for young children.

A full-day program allows teachers to increase outdoor time, choice time, art, and music. Most districts have additional expectations for full-day kindergartens. Some schools may emphasize writing while others may want this time devoted to math. Whatever this extra time is used for, we believe it is important that a full-day kindergarten does not become a mini first grade. We believe it is essential to use additional time in developmentally appropriate ways. Kindergarten teachers must be knowledgeable, well read, and up-to-date on current thinking and philosophy to stand up to these pressures. Knowledge is power.

Coming-in Time

Each day the children enter the classroom full of excitement and wonder. They find the hooks with their names and hang up their coats. Next, they take out any papers from their backpacks that they need to give to the teacher. At the beginning of the school year, we ask each child to bring a pocket folder to school to be used for papers coming to school and going home. On the first day of school we help each child trace her left hand on the left pocket and right hand on the right pocket. On the left we write "to school" and on the right, "going home." We try to establish good habits from the start.

We provide a basket for notes, books, and papers that don't need our attention immediately. After each child signs in or puts his name card up on the magnetic chalkboard (we use note cards with the children's names on the front and magnets on the back) or in a pocket chart, he is free to choose from a variety of activities until all the children arrive. Some days we put out specific tasks we would like the children to complete. It could be a graph where each student needs to write her name and put it in the column indicating how many people are in her family or estimating how many items are in a jar. Sometimes we will put out certain puzzles, math manipulatives, or simple board games or ask the children to cut out the monarch butterflies they painted the previous day. Often they are free to use the writing center or build with bristle blocks or Lego toys. We have found it's best not to take out things that require a time-consuming cleanup. Over the last few years, Debra has collaborated with fifth-grade teachers to have two students work with the kindergartners during coming-in time. They read to small groups, work on challenging puzzles, or help children that require one-to-one assistance on certain activities. The coming-in time is about twenty minutes and then we begin the Meeting and Greeting Circle.

Class Meeting

Pledge of Allegiance   Our days begin with the pledge. We realize reciting the Pledge of Allegiance is a controversial topic in some districts, but it is required where we teach. Children are expected to stand, put their right hands on their hearts, and recite the pledge. This routine can often take weeks to establish. First the children need to find their right hands and their hearts! Then the children need to learn the pledge. To add meaning to this exercise, we read the book *The Pledge of Allegiance* (2000), published by Scholastic. This book illustrates the concepts with photographs and can be a springboard to discussion. We hope this will provide some background and understanding as we recite the pledge each day.

Meeting and Greeting Circle   Most teachers begin the day with some type of meeting. We would like to share some of the features of our class meetings that have worked for us. Over the years we have struggled with having a circle versus having

Figure 2–1. Meeting and Greeting Circle

no circle. We feel it is important that children begin the day sitting in a circle looking at each other and greeting one another, but certain activities require that all the children face a bulletin board or chalkboard, and a circle can prevent everyone from being able to see. This is how we resolved it. We begin each session in a circle and welcome each other by having each child greet the person next to her. Sometimes we pass an object that might relate to a theme or shake hands or pass a small ball or hacky sack. On occasion, we ask each child to tell us something related to a theme or project as the students greet each other. We may ask each child to name a vegetable during a theme on food and nutrition or tell us his phone number or birthday when we are teaching that topic. On Chinese New Year, Bonnie taught the children to say "Happy New Year" in Chinese, and each child greeted the class with "Gung Hey Fat Choy." We may give each child a letter from the Chicka Chicka Boom Boom tree and ask each child to name his letter and place it on the tree as we go around the circle. Sometimes we play Who Stole the Cookies from the Cookie Jar or other name games. Learning each other's names, speaking loud enough to be heard, and looking at people as we greet them can take a while. We recommend reading *The Morning Meeting Book,* by Roxann Kriete (1999), to learn more about morning meetings. After greeting one another, Debra's children sing an opening song. Bonnie has the children begin their sharing.

Sharing   After everyone in the circle has greeted one another, each day four or five children share something they have made or brought to school that relates to the theme we are exploring. Speaking is one of the language arts, and this time gives each child an opportunity to practice speaking to the class. These sharing items remain in the classroom for the duration of the theme for other children to use. Typically, books, puzzles, toys, drawings, and other creations are shared. This adds some wonderful resources to our classroom during a theme. Sometimes we ask the children to share in a specific way. During a zoo theme, we may ask them each to bring a toy zoo animal in a bag and give three clues describing the animal. The rest of the class guesses until someone correctly identifies the animal in the bag. Sharing is also a chance for children to reveal talents and interests.

Another way to foster the home-school connection is through a traveling friend, Little Bear (this could be any stuffed animal or class mascot). Debra asks parents to record the bear's daily travels each evening in a small journal when their child brings him home. Little Bear commutes in a special tote bag along with a toothbrush and some great books about bears. She reads the short daily account of Little Bear's adventures at the class meeting.

We also share class-made big books that go home with a different child each evening. Parent comments are welcomed on a page at the end of the book and we share those comments at the class meeting. For the remaining portion of the class

Figure 2–2. Rachel shows a Monet print.

meeting, we ask the children to sit together on the rug and face the easel and bulletin board. This makes it possible for everyone to see.

Calendar   Next the calendar helper comes to the calendar and writes the number on the calendar. By changing the colors of the markers, we can teach patterns as we write the date each day. We begin with a basic AB pattern, using two alternating colors, and progress as the months pass to more advanced patterns, like AABC. We try to maximize this short segment and ask the children questions related to the calendar, such as "How many days until Bridget's birthday?" or "Who can tell me all the letters in *November?*" The calendar helper also asks his classmates a few questions. Learning to formulate and ask good questions is an important skill. We model this for the students and encourage them to take the pointer and ask their own questions. The calendar helper also checks the weather and records it on the Weather Graph. Another routine that helps children with counting and number understanding is

Figure 2–3. A calendar helper

counting the days of school to one hundred. Debra begins counting on the first day of school and Bonnie begins in January with the new calendar year. By putting a Popsicle stick in a box for each day and bundling them with a rubber band when there is a group of ten, we are laying the foundation for understanding place value. We also record the number for the day and make a number line to one hundred.

There are numerous resources dedicated entirely to ideas for calendar time. We have found it is best to try not to do too much. Instead we select a few routines that we feel teach skills that are best addressed during calendar time and expand and vary them as the year unfolds.

Daily Message   We write a daily message to the class on an eighteen-by-twenty-four-inch easel pad that tells the children something that will happen that day at school. Many literacy skills and concepts of print can be introduced and revisited during the message. As we write the message, the children are predicting and learning concepts of print, letters, words, sentences, punctuation, and symbol-sound association. This is a perfect time to do minilessons. Sometimes you can use an already written message and decode it and read it together, but we prefer to model the writing process on most days. Sometimes we omit words or letters and the children have to use different reading strategies to fill them in. Remembering that children are at varying levels in their literacy development, we address multiple levels as well as revisit skills and concepts day after day. Some children may be reading the entire message while others are just recognizing a few letters. Mostly, the children give responses as a group so no one is singled out. If we do ask individuals questions, we ask questions at their level. This way we can challenge some children and build confidence with others. We keep it lively and don't overdo it. We pay attention to the students. If they are not with us, it's time to stop. Early in the year, this activity may last only five to six minutes, but by spring, it may take twelve to fifteen minutes. It's the cumulative effect of doing the message day after day in these short segments that will make a difference in the children's literacy development.

We make the most of this message time by planning ahead. That way we know we are touching upon all the desired literacy skills and maintaining a logical and thorough progression. We are not suggesting that it is necessary to go in any specific order. For instance, we would not wait to learn words or talk about sentences and punctuation until children know all the letters. Children do not necessarily acquire skills and knowledge in a hierarchical progression, nor do they all learn it at the same rate or time. We need to revisit skills and concepts repeatedly and in different ways.

As we write the message, we like to think out loud by saying things like, "I'm leaving a space here because I'm making a new word," or "This is going to be a big word. Say the letters as I write them, k-i-n-d-e-r-g-a-r-t-n-e-r-s. Let's count the letters in that word." By having the children say the letters, we not only work on letter identification but also reinforce the concept of a letter. By asking them to count the letters in a word, we are letting them know that all those letters together make a word.

We keep the children actively involved by having them respond as a group or individually. Sometimes they come to the easel and point to a letter or word. We can learn so much by listening to the children's responses. While trying to teach rhyming recently, Bonnie used the word *make* in a sentence and then went back and showed the children how to create new words that rhyme with *make* by changing the initial consonant. Bonnie said, "If we change *m* to *r*, we have *rake*, and if we change *m* to *t*, we have *take*. If we change *m* to *l*, we have . . ." The children couldn't come up with the rhyming word, so Bonnie said, "We swim in the . . ." And they all called out "Pool!" The message here was we needed to do a bit more work on rhyming.

Figure 2–4. Reading the daily message

At the end of each week, Bonnie tears off that week's messages and staples them together to be placed in the classroom library. She refers to them as class newspapers and the children love to reread them during Relax and Read. If a child is celebrating a birthday, Bonnie writes a special message and draws a large birthday cake and candles. She tears off the birthday message for the student to take home that day. Then she writes a message that describes some of the day's activities. At the end of the school year, she gives each child a class newspaper to take home.

Music and Movement

This is one of our favorite times of the day. There are a number of things we can do during Music and Movement but we always make sure the children get an opportunity to be up and moving. One way we use this time is to teach and sing songs related to a theme or topic that we are currently exploring. For example, in January it is a great time to teach songs about the months of the year and days of the week. During a fairy tale theme, we sing "Fairy Tales Are Wonderful" and "Fairy Tales, Fairy Tales." As our song and dance repertoire grows, we revisit the good old favorites. Children love to return to the familiar and sing songs from earlier months and themes.

Our children enjoy many dances. One of our favorites is "Jump Jim Joe." This is a very basic song and dance included on a CD by the same name (New England

Dancing Masters 1991). Greg and Steve (1987, 1997, 2000) also have many dances that are easy to learn as the children listen to the CDs.

And of course, there are numerous songs that have been made into picture books. It is helpful to teach new songs with these picture books because they provide illustrations that help the children understand and learn the songs. We have included a list of our favorite song books as well as CDs and artists we recommend in the appendix.

We always try to select high-quality, original music. We also expose children to a range of music, such as folk, jazz, classical, peppy, and peaceful. We suggest investing in a CD player if you're still using tapes. It provides better-quality sound and makes it much quicker to find a particular song. We even have a remote control that can be very handy as we jive about the classroom.

It has been our experience that some children are slow to warm up and sing and dance in a group. We respect that and let children join in when they are ready. Most children jump in quickly, but if a child needs more time to become comfortable, we are patient with him.

Figure 2–5. Music and Movement

It seems the days of kindergarten teachers playing the piano is a thing of the past. But with a CD player we can now expose children to a wider range of wonderful music by the original artists. We've known a few kindergarten teachers who feel uncomfortable singing and dancing. We think that a good music program is just as important as any other subject area. Not only are there language and literacy benefits as children see the words to songs on charts and in books and discover the rhyme and rhythm of language, but we are laying a foundation for a life filled with the joy of music. Neither of us will win any prizes singing or dancing with adults, but our kindergartners think we are very cool. And that's all that matters.

We also invite family members that play musical instruments to visit and share their talents. We are fortunate that our schools provide cultural arts events that expose the children to different types of music. And we invite the older students in the school to play for us. These are often older siblings or friends and having them in our classrooms is very exciting.

We like to have our students create songbooks. As we teach the children new songs each week, we give them each a page with the words to the song and have

Figure 2–6. Illustrating our songbooks

them illustrate the song. We keep these pages in small three-ring binders, and at the end of the year, each child has an illustrated collection of all the songs she's learned in kindergarten. This is also a literacy activity as the children begin to read words in the songs.

Following are some of our favorite (and our children's favorite) CDs and the specific songs we use as well.

Dancing and Movement

Big Fun (Greg and Steve 1997)
   The Mack Chicken Dance
   The Movement Medley
   New Zoo Review
   Party Line

Kids in Action (Greg and Steve 2000)
   Beanie Bag Dance
   Drop Till You Bop
   Get Ready Get Set Let's Dance

Kids in Motion (Greg and Steve 1987)
   Bean Bag Boogie
   Freeze Dance
   Kids in Motion
   The Body Rock
   Animal Action II

Blue Sky City (Skip West 1999)
   Kids Like to Boogie Too
   We All Get Up in the Morning

Down in the Valley book and CD (New England Dancing Masters 2000)
   At the Bottom of the Sea
   Chee Chee Cha
   Charlie Over the Ocean
   Gramma Moses
   Hambone (use with book *Hush Little Baby*, by Marla Frazee [1999])
   Hunt the Cows
   The Tree Song

Jump Jim Joe CD and book (New England Dancing Masters 1991)
   Jump Jim Joe

Dr. Jean Sings Silly Songs (Dr. Jean 2001)
   Cool Bear Hunt

Sing to Learn (Dr. Jean 2000)
   Macarena Math

Dr. Jean and Friends (Dr. Jean 1998)
    Macarena Months
    Tooty Ta
Is Everybody Happy? (Dr. Jean 2001)
    Lettercize
Rock n' Roll Songs That Teach (The Learning Station 1997)
    Singin' in the Rain
    Rock n' Roll Journey
All-Time Favorite Dances (Kimbo Educational 1991)
Chimes of Dunkirk: Teaching Dance to Children DVD, book, and CD (New England Dancing Masters 2003)

Singing

Teaching Kindergarten (Mary Alice Amidon 1992) (All of the songs on these two CDs were selected for a theme-based kindergarten curriculum that Bonnie coauthored.)
We All Sing with the Same Voice book and CD (Phillip Miller and Sheppard Greene 1982) (great to sing and sign)
We All Live Together, Volume 1 (Greg and Steve 1983)
    ABC Rock
We All Live Together, Volume 2 (Greg and Steve 1987)
    Good Morning
    The Number Rock
    Months of the Year
    The World Is a Rainbow
Big Fun (Greg and Steve 1997)
    The Magic of Reading
This Pretty Planet—Songs for the Earth (The Amidons 1990)
I'll Never Forget (The Amidons 1993)
Things Are Going My Way—Traditional Songs for Children (The Amidons 1984) (see *www.amidonmusic.com* for information on their CDs)
Keep on Singing and Dancing (Dr. Jean 1999)
    Alphabet Forwards and Backwards
    Peanut Butter
Dr. Jean Sings Silly Songs (Dr. Jean 2001)
    Baby Fish
    Katilina Matilina
Dr. Jean and Friends (Dr. Jean 1998)
    Patalina Matalina
Hello World (Red Grammer 1995)
    On the Day You Were Born (wonderful birthday song)

Teaching Peace (Red Grammer 1986)
    I Think You're Wonderful
    Rapp Song
    Hooray for the World

Read-Aloud

This is the time when we read to the children. It can be nonfiction that relates to our theme or project, shared reading with a big book, or a work of fiction. Reading aloud well to children is a real skill. We prefer to preview books before reading to the class. That way we can plan before reading. We might pose a question or two we want the children to think about while listening to the story. Sometimes a word might need to be defined or background information presented prior to reading a book. Or we might develop a few questions to generate some discussion about the characters, setting, or plot. Also, there may be subject matter that is inappropriate or the book may not be worth reading. There is so much good literature available that there's no need to waste time on anything mediocre. A few years ago we attended the New England Kindergarten Conference in Providence, Rhode Island, and heard Mem Fox speak. Mem is an author of many popular children's books and she is also a former professor of literacy education. She lives in Adelaide, Australia. She spoke of the importance of reading aloud well to children. A point that stayed with us was that it's beneficial to read the ending of a story slowly and in particular to pause at the last page and through the last words. This allows the children to reflect a bit on the story. We recommend her book *Reading Magic* (2001). Reading aloud well to children requires practice. It takes some time to develop one's own style.

    We select a range of different books to read so the children are exposed to many genres and authors over the course of the year. This is one of those routines that can make a powerful impact over time. At the very least, we try to read two books per day to the children. Over the course of a school year, that's approximately 360 books!

Relax and Read

After we read to the children, we give them about ten minutes to relax with a friend on a beanbag chair, lie on the rug, or sit at the table and enjoy some self-selected books. We try to be well prepared for center time so we can relax and read with the children. This is a time when we can begin to develop enthusiasm for reading and nurture a positive disposition for literacy. We can expose children to the world of books by taking the time to find and display books in centers and on bookshelves and change them often to strengthen the children's interest in reading.

    There is nothing quite as rewarding as hearing one child retell Dr. Seuss' *Red Fish Blue Fish* while looking at the pictures and turning the pages, another pair

Figure 2–7. Relax and Read

of children rereading *Brown Bear, Brown Bear,* which was a shared reading earlier in the week, and another small group discussing the pictures while studying a nonfiction book on bats. By modeling our love of books and providing a rich and varied assortment of books all year long, we have the ability to develop positive attitudes toward books and reading that last a lifetime.

Center Time/Choice Time

There are different names for this portion of the day and many ways to approach it, but the important thing is that the children are engaged in developmentally appropriate activities for about an hour. In Debra's class, the teacher and assistant work with some students in small groups while other children are independently engaged in a variety of activities such as painting, playing at the rice table, using math manipulatives, building with blocks, and participating in dramatic play. Two of Debra's center time activities are guided by teachers, assistants, or volunteers. At the guided centers children do activities such as writing, collaborative class books, sketching the life cycle of a butterfly, and playing a math game. Bonnie's center time is slightly different. She plans three different activities each day and the children rotate through all three activities in small groups. She plans activities from different areas of the curriculum and includes a balance of quiet and more active centers. She usually leads the activity where a new concept is being

Figure 2–8. Center time activities

taught or where her expertise is needed most. Parent volunteers lead the other activities. Center activities could include math games, book extensions, painting, sketching, block building, and dramatic play. The possibilities are limited only by one's creativity and energy. Bonnie begins choice time after the planned center time activities. At choice time, children are free to select their own activities.

By having children work in small groups at center time, it is possible to challenge children who are ready and to provide further instruction for those who need it. Vygotsky said that children's higher mental functions have their roots in social interaction and collaborative activities. Vygotsky also taught us that children can reach for higher levels of social and cognitive functioning in a social support system, for example constructive play groups and guided groups. Vygotsky described this concept of stretching to higher levels as working in one's *zone of proximal development*.

Snack

We want to provide time for a snack but do not want it to take a disproportionate amount of time. Debra's children are free to eat snacks during center time.

Bonnie puts a snack out after the children have finished center time and move into choice time.

One option is to have children take turns bringing a snack for the entire class. With an increase in serious allergies, prepackaged graham crackers or granola bars that list their ingredients are fine, or snacks can be limited to veggies and fruits. Bonnie has switched to fruits and vegetables only this year and recommends it. The children are eating much healthier snacks, trying new things, and eating more than when snacks were predominantly carbohydrates. Another option is for each child to bring a light, healthful snack from home. Snacks can be enjoyed at a table where a small group can socialize while eating. This is a good opportunity to facilitate social skills and, if time allows, to sit at the snack table with the children. Bonnie worked with a wonderful special education teacher that used snack and choice time to teach social skills.

Figure 2–9. Fruit for snack

Cleanup

We communicate clear expectations to our children about cleanup time. We take the time to show the children how to put things away. The organization established in September helps the children take responsibility for putting things away in their places. Blocks of the same shape are put together on the shelves, modelling dough is placed in the sealed plastic containers, wooden train tracks are carefully stacked in a large basket, and so on.

As children finish putting away all the toys and other materials, warm soapy sponges are available to wash the tables. Children also find a partner and clean the floor with small brooms and dust pans. We have some colleagues that use upbeat Motown music to motivate the children at cleanup time. Whatever gets them going!

Bonnie has two students from fifth grade come at the end of each day to wash tables and put up chairs. They also tidy the shelves and put away anything the kindergartners may have missed. Not only is this great for the kindergarten teacher, but the older children love coming back to help. These are highly sought after jobs. It took Bonnie twenty-five years to think of this and she stumbled upon the idea quite by accident, but she highly recommends it.

As children finish cleaning up they should know where to go and what to do since this has the potential to be a difficult transition time. Relax and Read or a song is a way to refocus children as they finish cleaning up.

Outside Play

Here in the Northeast, winters can be harsh and frequently it is too cold or snowy to get outside. So when the weather is pleasant, it is a real treat to run outdoors and play. Outdoor playtime helps our active kindergartners release some of their energy. The children use their muscles and enjoy a different type of play. As winter progresses, it often becomes difficult for the active students to control their energy and stay focused during the morning meeting and center times. We all begin to get cabin fever! If we lived in a milder climate, we would be outside each and every day. There is more about outside play in the May chapter.

Closing

We think it is important to reconvene as a group before leaving for the day. This is the time to read an additional book and perhaps share some of the children's writing or drawings or allow some of the students to share their work or discoveries made at center time that day. Debra likes to end with a good-bye song as well. We hand out any papers that need to go home at this time and then we pack up and get on the jackets. As winter approaches we need to leave extra time for boots, snowsuits,

Figure 2–10. Outdoor play

mittens, hats, and scarves. We encourage the children to put on as much of their outdoor clothing themselves as possible. We also suggest some practice at home.

Communication

Communication is a critical component of a successful early childhood program. Not only is it important for us to communicate our philosophy, schedules, and expectations to the families, but we try to be sensitive to the needs and cultures of the students and families. We believe communication goes both ways. September is the time we explain to our parents how we will communicate with them and how best to communicate with us. Here are several ways we communicate with our families.

Parent Handbook

We both have developed a Parent Handbook. It is a good way to explain our philosophies and routines and let parents know exactly what to expect in kindergarten. We give the handbooks to parents during the first visit to school in the fall so they will have time to read them before Open House. Writing these handbooks has helped us reflect on our programs and articulate our curricula, philosophy, and routines.

Conferences, Phone Calls, and Email

We have regularly scheduled conferences (they are described in detail in the November chapter) and invite parents to request a meeting whenever they have a concern. We tell parents in September that we welcome their phone calls and emails and will respond as quickly as possible. This is often a family's first experience with school and we want to be responsive to their questions and concerns.

Newsletters

We recommend sending a newsletter every week or biweekly. Throughout the week we compile a list of things to include in the newsletter. Then when we sit down to write the newsletter it's much quicker. We compose our newsletters on the computer and they can be as simple or as elaborate as time and talent permit. We like to include photographs that we have taken with a digital camera. The newsletter includes things we have done in class during the week, items children will need to bring to school, special events, and anything we want to communicate to parents.

Website

A website can include children's art, volunteer schedules, snack schedules, articles for parents to read, and more extensive information about curriculum. For safety reasons, we do not include photos of the children or last names on artwork. At this point in time, some of our parents do not have Internet access, so if we have information that all parents must receive, we include it in a newsletter. We have gotten feedback from grandparents throughout the country who enjoy our websites and especially the children's art.

Volunteering

Another way to communicate with parents is by inviting them to volunteer in the classroom on a regular basis or visit as their schedules permit. Parents who are curious about the day-to-day operations of the kindergarten classroom will get an education by helping in the classroom. We find parents have great respect for the role of a kindergarten teacher after spending time in our classrooms.

These are some ways to communicate with parents in kindergarten. We have found that many children and parents are anxious as they enter kindergarten.

Figure 2–11. Parent volunteer having blood pressure taken.

We want to communicate in a way that will help alleviate anxiety and inspire confidence. Remembering that effective communication is a two-way street, we want to be receptive and let parents know they are being heard. Being good listeners can be as important as explaining our programs and philosophies.

Open House or Back to School Night

Different schools use various names for these special events, but we are referring to the evening when parents come to school (without children) and go to their child's classroom to learn about the program and philosophy of the school and teacher. This usually occurs in September or early October. It is our opportunity to articulate our goals for the kindergarten program and create a warm and collaborative relationship with parents.

Some ways to stay focused and get important points across are to use the overhead projector, large charts, a PowerPoint presentation, or slides to provide a framework for sharing important information. A video that showcases students and their work is a great addition to a presentation by the teacher.

There will also be several "housekeeping" items to cover, such as information about conferences, birthdays, and volunteering in the classroom. The majority of our presentation relates to the curriculum, the district's philosophy, and our personal philosophy and how we will implement it.

Open House is also a time to ask parents to sign up to volunteer in the classroom, for parent-teacher conferences, and to contribute to classroom celebrations. The specific routines will vary from school to school, but we have sign-up sheets ready for this evening that are clearly labeled for whatever we'd like parents to do. Teachers that have A.M. and P.M. classes can color-code them. Some of the sign-ups that we find useful are

- conferences
- guest readers

Figure 2–12. Quotes representing our philosophy for Open House

- special talents—musicians, doctors/nurses, artists, etc. (We think about the topics that we will be exploring and try to recruit parents with related skills and talents.)
- classroom volunteers
- parties/celebrations (This a great time to ask parents if they can help with snacks, drinks, and supplies for celebrations throughout the year. As party time approaches, we just ask our room mom or dad to call and remind people of what they volunteered to bring for that celebration.)
- other jobs (These are other jobs we find help the classroom run smoothly: sewing, repairing items, shopping, covering books with contact paper.)

Open House is a time to display some of the children's work as well. We are careful that all the children are equally represented and organize the classroom so it reflects our philosophy and how much we care about the children. We want to make the most of this opportunity!

Names, Names, Names!

Using students' names at the beginning of school is a natural way to begin developing early literacy skills. The first word most children read and write is their name. Here are some of the ways we have used the children's names early in the year.

Letter by Letter

We write each child's name on a flashcard. We start by using first names only and later add last names. We put these names in a sleeve (this is essentially a long envelope with an opening on one end) that we either purchased or made by folding and taping a large rectangle out of tagboard or construction paper. We can use this set of name cards to transition to an activity or dismiss the children from a group. They have to look carefully for their own name as we slowly slide a child's name card from the sleeve. As the first letter of a name emerges from the sleeve, there is often more than one guess if there are students whose names start with the same letter. The children need to discriminate between two similar names, such as Bryan and Bridget or Julia and Jonathan, based on the second or third letter. As the year progresses and the children get better at reading first names, Debra provides a challenge by including last names.

Name Bingo

We play bingo using the children's names. We simply print all the children's names on sentence strips or oak-tag cards in advance. It's best to play this game in a small group of five to eight children. Taking turns, each child chooses a letter

Figure 2–13. Debra pulls out a name letter by letter.

from a box and identifies it. (Bonnie did a variation of this game by using the Chicka Chicka Boom Boom Tree and putting the letters on the tree as we called them out.) If any child has that letter in his name, he places a penny or counter on that letter on his name card. The first child to cover all the letters in her name shouts out "Bingo!" (or "Chicka Chicka Boom Boom!"). Children can trade name cards and play again to learn additional letters.

Attendance Names

We want the children to be responsible for taking attendance right from the beginning of the year. We take digital photos of each child and print and mount each on a piece of oak tag or construction paper. We write the child's name under the photo and laminate the card or cover it with contact paper. On the back we stick a magnet. As each child enters the class, he finds his name and picture and places it in a basket or box to show he is present. Alternatively the name cards can be spread out on a table and each child can place her card on a magnetic chalkboard upon entering the classroom. Later in the day the teacher can use these name cards to divide the children into activity groups. After a month or so, we replace these name cards with ones that do not have photos. Debra even moves to using only last names on these cards. In February, after the

Figure 2–14. Bonnie plays name bingo.

children have worked on Valentines, we ask each child individually to try to read her classmates' names. We record the results and this becomes one more indicator when assessing reading progress.

Beanie Names

We write large letters (about three inches high) for each of our kindergartners' names on heavy tagboard or cardboard. (We have found framing shops will donate scraps of matte board that are excellent for this.) We provide an assortment of beans and seeds in shallow bowls (recycled margarine containers or plastic chip and dip platters work well for this). Then we have the children put glue on one letter at a time and place the beans on each letter as they go along. These names are great to reuse during the year as a way to identify student work on a bulletin board or help any children who are struggling with learning to write or recognize their names. We have one piece of advice: if you have a mouse problem in the classroom, hang these cards on the walls instead of laying them on a table or countertop.

Figure 2–15. Count the Letters in Your Name Graph

Count the Letters in Your Name Graph

At the beginning of the year we can teach letter identification by selecting one child's name card out of a can each day. After making a quick prediction as to how many letters there will be in *Maurice*, for example, the children count the letters and then Maurice cuts apart his name card and glues it letter by letter in the column for names having seven letters. The large graph takes a little bit of planning by the teacher. You need to lay out the students' names from shortest to longest and then create a column for each number of letters. You also need to have a set of name cards prepared to cut apart. If you do one child's name each day, it will take several weeks to complete the graph, but it is an excellent way to teach letter recognition and help children begin reading each other's names.

Boy/Girl Chart

Prepare a large piece of chart paper with a centerline. Label one side of the chart "boys" and the other "girls." Have each child complete a square by drawing a picture of his or her face and writing his or her name and then gluing it to the appropriate side of the chart. We usually do this chart the second or third day of school since it is very basic (see p. 50). We don't even put the pictures in any organized

Figure 2–16. Boy/Girl Chart

rows but just on the correct side of the centerline. We use the completed graph at our morning meeting as a minilesson for math. A variation on this activity is to sometimes ask the children to put up their name cards to make a boy/girl chart as they enter the classroom.

Birthday Graph

We prepare a graph that has twelve columns and print the names of the months at the bottom of each column. Then we have each child fill out a small square with his name and perhaps a birthday icon such as a cake or a candle or balloons. We write the child's birth date (unless she knows it) next to her name. We have each child put his name in the appropriate column on the birthday graph and use this graph at the morning meeting. We talk about the results—which months have the most or least birthdays and so on. We hang this graph in a place where we can refer to it throughout the year.

Reading All Around

Throughout this book we address reading much like we do in the classroom. It is difficult to put it all in one chapter because we teach reading at many different times of the day and in many different ways. We integrate reading into nearly everything we do. Most of the time the children don't realize we are doing reading in the way they know we are doing writing. When children write they are encoding and need to make a deliberate effort to do so. They have to pick up a pencil or marker and write something on the paper. In the early stages, kindergartners' writing is typically drawing. With reading it's a bit more subtle. Children are trying to make meaning of all those strange marks they see everywhere. We help them get meaning from print.

We approach this from many different directions. We teach children to identify letters and their corresponding sounds. This happens when we play letter recognition games and when a child writes a patient's history in the dramatic play area. We teach children to read whole words by reading short, leveled books and placing labels around the classroom. We teach children vocabulary and the language of books when we read aloud to them each day. We teach children to use syntax clues when we write and read the daily message together. We teach them about picture clues and semantic clues when we read big books. We identify many ways in which we create a literate environment throughout this book. We don't believe kindergartners should be learning to read through reading groups and seatwork. That's why we couldn't tie it all up in a neat little chapter; instead, we sprinkled it throughout the book just as we sprinkle it throughout the kindergarten day.

Write at the Start

In our kindergartens, we weave writing into many parts of our programs: the morning message, book extensions, dramatic play, theme work, projects, and anywhere we see a reason or opportunity for writing. We refer to this as integrated writing. Writers workshop is another component of our writing program and we do this during a designated time period. The two are quite different in some ways but both are important to our programs and designed to help the children see writing as a natural extension to listening, speaking, reading, representing, and viewing. We have sprinkled ideas for integrating writing throughout this book. As we describe a particular theme, project, dramatic play, or center activity, we will make specific references to integrated writing.

Writers workshop is a very specific way of engaging children in writing and we recommend that you read about writers workshop in more detail or attend some workshops to understand it thoroughly before implementing it in your kindergarten. We currently do writers workshop and integrate writing throughout the day.

Many kindergarten teachers in our area have had the good fortune to work over the past few years with an outstanding writing instructor, Leah Mermelstein. She has instructed and coached us on using kindergarten writers workshop. This workshop time has become important as a way for our kindergartners to grow as writers. The writers workshop has a predictable structure. When we do writers workshop, it looks like this:

- The children gather on the rug and sit next to their "talking partners" (two children teamed up to share and discuss concepts presented in a minilesson).
- During the minilesson we purposefully and a bit dramatically talk to the children about the concept we want to teach. An example of a minilesson about staying on the topic could be writing and drawing about a trip to the beach. On about page 3 of our large demonstration story, we could interject a non sequitur such as "I can't wait for my birthday." Then we can ask the class, "Did this go with my story about my summer vacation?" After this mishap, we quickly write the rest of the story appropriately on the topic.
- The children practice the concept we have presented by talking to their partners. For example, we might ask each team of talking partners to think of an important or memorable topic to write about. Then the students would turn to their partners and share their ideas and listen to their partners' story. The children are then ready to leave the writing meeting and each has a definite topic for starting a new story (if he has completed all the existing pieces in his writing folder).
- Children work on their writing (we conference with a few children per day at this time).
- We all gather for a brief sharing of selected children's pieces that highlight skills taught in today's and previous writing lessons.

Naturally, as the year unfolds, we expect the children's writing to move along a developmental continuum. A progression of writing expectations and skill development would look something like this during the fall:

- Children share stories primarily through their drawings.
- Children begin adding more details in their drawings.
- Some children use scribbles or random letters to go with their illustrations.
- Some children write initial letters for words.

- Children generally use unlined paper or more than one line on lined paper because they do not have a sense of the lines or spaces.

If children can tell a story through their pictures and some small bits of writing, this is very good work for the fall. For many children, personal narrative is natural at this time of year. A good way to help children write personal narrative is to ask the children to write a lot about something they know. Some of our opening writers workshop minilessons have modeled writing passionately about things you know a lot about. Jonathan London's book *What Do You Love?* (2000) is a great book to use for this concept. A friend of ours, also a kindergarten teacher, shared a funny and unusual story about one of her little boys. After hearing one day's mini writing lesson, he wrote a story titled "All About Flushing a Toilet." He certainly got the concept of writing about "something you know a lot about."

Nonfiction is also a good way to begin writers workshop in the fall. In fact, for many children, it is easier to write about things and experiences they know

Figure 2–17. Fall writing sample: "One time my dog had a seizure on vacation. I was at Maine," by Leah.

53

about firsthand. For the child who has a collection or love of a sport, this can be the basis for strong writing.

In a full-day kindergarten program, writers workshop might last twenty to forty minutes, three or four days a week, with shorter sessions in the fall and longer ones in the late winter and spring. In a half-day program, realistically, writers workshop can take place two or three days a week for twenty to thirty minutes. This still allows enough time for the other curricular demands and enough quality playtime.

Dramatic Play

Our kindergarten classrooms have an area set aside for dramatic play. As the standards have been raised and pressures to achieve have been pushed down to kindergarten, we have seen kindergartens without a dramatic play area and even without blocks. We firmly believe it is our responsibility as early childhood

Figure 2–18. Children in dramatic play area

educators to keep our classrooms developmentally appropriate while meeting the standards. The two are not mutually exclusive!

We begin the year with a house set up in the dramatic play area, but we do change this area as the year progresses to enhance our themes or project work. We try to provide as many opportunities as possible for literacy and math through dramatic play. One successful play environment is a kindergarten café. The children make menus, take orders, collect money, and put it in the cash register. Of course, charging something is always an option. There are many ways to set up the dramatic play area to encourage social collaboration, foster language development, provide play to reinforce learning, and give children a chance to just have fun.

We have found the play to be more productive if we take time to teach the children how to use props when a new dramatic play area is set up. Doing this in groups of about six or seven works best. Early this year, Bonnie was working with a small group of children at the writing table and in her peripheral vision, she noticed a small plastic head of lettuce being flung across the classroom. She realized she needed to do some reteaching about the appropriate way to play in the dramatic play area. She also had a little chat with the parents of the child who sent the lettuce flying. The next day he came to school and handed Bonnie a note saying,

Figure 2–19. Sean and Brendan make a shopping list before visiting the classroom grocery store.

"I am sorry. It will not happen again." And it hasn't. It pays to address behavior like this right away because children often test the limits in a new setting.

We have used the dramatic play area in many different ways. During a theme on bones and skeletons, we created a hospital complete with X rays on the windows, medical charts on the wall, a model of a human skeleton, gowns for surgery, a homemade X-ray machine, plenty of bandages, casts, and medical equipment to deal with anything from broken bones to childbirth. Yes, it's true. We have seen the children use a naked baby doll to represent a newborn. Clipboards to chart the patient's progress and small papers to write prescriptions help integrate writing.

Grocery store, bakery, post office, farm stand, school, veterinarian's office, fairy tale or nursery rhyme theater, shoe store, and pizza parlor are a few other favorite setups for the dramatic play area.

Art: Something to Think About

Our kindergartners do not receive art instruction from a trained art teacher. Some full-day kindergartners do work with an art teacher once a week. In either situation, we believe we are responsible for the majority of art instruction because art is best integrated into the daily curriculum. Art can be integrated with reading, writing, math, science, social studies, and music. Kindergartners should have opportunities to explore, experiment, and create in some way each day. We want to send a message to the children that we value their creativity and they are free to use various materials.

We are careful to teach the children how to use and care for the materials so they can be used and enjoyed with independence throughout the year. We demonstrate various techniques with different activities like water painting, splattering, rubbings, and crayon resist. We provide opportunities for the children to draw, paint, or do an art project related to a particular theme or topic. We encourage children to explore and experiment with materials and have fun. We usually steer clear of patterns to be traced and step-by-step craft projects in which each child's work ends up looking very much the same as everyone else's. We don't want children to think there is a right way to do art. We want them to make choices and create something that is their own.

Some teachers are intimidated when teaching art. Perhaps they do not feel properly trained in this area or think they are not creative or artistic themselves. All teachers can provide children with opportunities to be creative and explore different media. By asking yourself a few simple questions, it is easy to provide young children with developmentally appropriate art experiences.

Figure 2–20. Children paint at a large wall easel.

Figure 2–21. Children paint at a table.

- *Have you spent more time preparing this activity than it will take the children to complete it?* If your answer is yes, then chances are you have done too much of the work. You may have created things for students to trace or have done so much preparation that it has become your project rather than theirs. The best art projects generally start with a blank piece of paper or a blob of clay.
- *When the children have completed their projects, do they all look alike?* If your projects are open-ended and children have the freedom to create, the final products will look different. As a teacher becomes familiar with each child's painting and drawing styles, he will be able to identify many of the artists in the class without even looking at the names.
- *Did you reproduce copies of this activity on a copier? Are the children required to cut on dotted lines or color in predrawn pictures or shapes? Are they using tracers?* We don't consider these activities art because they don't let the children make choices or express their creativity and individuality.

There are occasions when it is appropriate to guide the art project, but it is definitely the exception and not the rule. For example, recently Bonnie's children worked on an activity involving coloring the various characters in *The Mitten*, by Jan Brett. By making copies, Bonnie provided each child with labeled pictures of all of the characters. She then asked the children to take the colored pictures home and retell the story to their families while using one of their own mittens. The emphasis on this activity was retelling, and by giving the children the pre-drawn characters to color, Bonnie made sure they all had identifiable characters that did not take days to create.

Another occasion when a more structured art activity was appropriate was in the fall, during a theme on monarch butterflies. Bonnie gives each child a pre-traced outline of a butterfly on a piece of eleven-by-fourteen-inch paper. After teaching the children about monarchs and symmetry, she gives them orange, black, and white paint and asks them to paint monarchs. By tracing an outline for each child, Bonnie ensures they will have enough space to demonstrate their understanding of symmetry. And her classroom will be filled with large, colorful monarch butterflies.

Building Blocks: Don't Start Kindergarten Without Them

We believe that no kindergarten classroom should be without blocks. This may sound strident but there is nothing that integrates all curriculum areas and fosters social development better than blocks. The beauty of blocks is they are open-ended and the children have complete control in the design and creation. Block building allows the children opportunities to think, plan, pose questions, and collabora-tively solve problems.

Building with blocks enhances learning in all the major curriculum areas. In science, a block builder learns about gravity, balance, stability, weight, and incline planes. Builders also learn about trial and error. In the area of math, the child learns about classification, patterns, symmetry, order, numbers, fractions, depth, width, height, length, measurement, and area. Physical development improves and muscles are strengthened while students carry blocks to a construction site and then again at cleanup. In language development, the children learn much about directions, labeling, signs, and the use of prepositions such as *over, under, through,* and *upon.* The children use much language by asking questions, exchang-ing ideas, and making up rich stories about their buildings. Lastly, the blocks do much to strengthen children's social capabilities. They learn to listen to other children and share ideas. They also learn to take turns with coveted toys, cooperate while building, work hard during cleanup, and they build feelings of competence and pride through their constructions.

After taking a couple of months to settle in, we allow the children to keep buildings standing and add to them the next day. Signs on buildings help other children respect what is being built. Other children can either add their ideas

Figure 2–22. Proud builders

carefully or begin their own building. When cleanup is necessary, snapping a few photographs of the buildings helps the children let go of their great constructions. Cleanup of blocks in Debra's room is usually on Fridays. An exception to that rule is during project work when the class adds to the block structure each day over the course of the entire project. Even after project work is completed a block structure may stay up a while longer to facilitate extended dramatic play.

In addition to unit blocks, large hollow-core blocks are appropriate, and the children love them. We house both types of blocks in our block areas. Small props such as people, animals, cars, road signs, and various small tabletop blocks allow for rich play.

Teachers who do not have blocks because their school cannot afford to buy them may want to think about putting together a proposal to the school's parent-teacher association, the board of education, the principal, the local chamber of commerce, or other area organizations. You can purchase blocks over time, starting with a smaller set the first year and adding to the set each year. Once they are obtained they last for generations.

Summary

The highlight in September is that the children have arrived. They give focus and meaning to all that we planned in August. Being a teacher is a good deal like conducting an orchestra. The orchestra brings the conductor's planning and preparation to life. And, for us, it is the children that give meaning to all we do.

With a well-thought-out schedule and routines that are clearly and patiently demonstrated, September becomes an exciting start to the year. Our kindergartners arrive with a wide range of developmental levels and experiences, and the start of school is an easier transition for some children than for others. But in time, all the children adjust to their new environment, make friends, and become comfortable with their teachers.

After many years of teaching, we have come to realize that it is important to start slowly and thoughtfully. We begin with only a few important routines and play areas open to the children. We add others slowly and try to be clear about our expectations and take the time that is required for the children to be successful. This practice contributes greatly to a smooth start to the new school year for us and the children.

We know kindergarten is a big transition for four- and five-year-olds from preschools, day care centers, and pre-K classes where there are fewer children and more adults.

Good Books for Starting the Year

Bang, M. 1999. *When Sophie Gets Angry—Really, Really Angry*. New York: Blue Sky.

Barrett, J. 1998. *Things That Are Most in the World*. New York: Atheneum Books for Young Readers.

Bourgeois, P. 1995. *Franklin Goes to School*. New York: Scholastic.

Brown, M. 1995. *Arthur Goes to School*. New York: Random House.

Carlson, N. 1994. *How to Lose All Your Friends*. New York: Viking.

———. 1999. *Look Out Kindergarten, Here I Come*. New York: Puffin.

Cheltenham Elementary School Kindergartners. 1991. *We Are All Alike . . . We Are All Different*. New York: Scholastic.

Civardi, A., and S. Cartwright. 1985. *Going to School*. England: Usborne.

Danneberg, J. 2000. *First Day Jitters*. Cambridge, MA: Charlesbridge.

Ehlert, L. 1990. *Feathers for Lunch*. New York: Trumpet Club.

Emberly, E. 1992. *Go Away Big Green Monster*. New York: Little, Brown.

Howe, J. 1986. *When You Go to Kindergarten*. New York: Mulberry.

London, J. 1996. *Froggy Goes to School*. New York: Scholastic.

Marzollo, J. 1995. *I Spy School Days*. New York: Scholastic.

Miller, J. P., and S. M. Greene. 1982. *We All Sing with the Same Voice*. New York: Harper Collins.

Rogers, J. 2002. *Kindergarten*. New York: Scholastic.

Senisi, E. 1994. *Kindergarten Kids*. New York: Scholastic.

Shannon, D. 1998. *No, David!* New York: Blue Sky.

———. 1999. *David Goes to School*. New York: Blue Sky.

——— 2002. *David Gets in Trouble*. New York: Blue Sky.

Slate, J. 1996. *Miss Bindergarten Goes to Kindergarten*. New York: Dutton.

Weiss, G. D., and B. Thiele. 1995. *What a Wonderful World*. New York: Atheneum Books for Young Readers.

October

Getting to Know You

In October the children have learned how the classroom works and are inter-acting more comfortably and capably with peers. We are in the routine, so to speak.

Now we are working to refine procedures and teach independence. The children are better able to share and play cooperatively. We have shown the children some turn-taking strategies and the children with stronger social skills are modeling cooperative behavior.

We are involved in themes and projects and the children are excited about learning. They have already shown more interest and progress in drawing and writing. It is exciting to have a new group of students off to a good start. As for us, we are no longer completely exhausted by the end of the week. Some social life returns to our Friday evenings.

Evaluation

We are getting to know the children and are taking anecdotal records and beginning to do assessment in preparation for November conferences with parents. Throughout the school year we use these basic types of assessments: formative, summative, and program evaluation. Formative assessment helps us determine where each child is in different areas of her development so we can provide appropriate experiences, activities, and assistance. Summative assessment gives us information to share with parents, the school district, and first-grade teachers. Program evaluation lets us know how well our program meets the needs of the students, the parents, and the school.

Formative Assessment

Anecdotal Records   Many of the decisions we make about day-to-day instruction and activities are based on abilities the children demonstrate. We gather this information in a variety of ways. One of the most useful and natural ways to learn about each child's development in different areas is by making anecdotal records. We like to target one activity to observe each week. For instance, we may observe the children while building with blocks to learn about their social development or observe the children counting objects to assess one-to-one correspondence. By observing a child doing a variety of activities, over time we get a good picture of the child's overall development. We record these observations on a very basic and open-ended record form that we make by dividing an 8½-by-14-inch piece of paper into rectangles (one for each child) and jotting our observations in each space. At the top of each form we write the activity we are observing and the date. It is easier to fit all the children on one side of the paper if we use the larger paper. This is much simpler than flipping the page over to find a child's name. This information is valuable when doing reports and having conferences. Parents appreciate examples when we relate information about their child. And it gives us more credibility if we can be specific when talking to parents.

Sometimes we need specific information about one particular child, and anecdotal records are useful for this too. For instance, a child may be having difficulty interacting with peers. Taking five minutes to observe this child as she plays and record our observations can be very helpful. We repeat this in different settings to identify the problem and determine where to begin in our efforts to help this child interact more appropriately with peers.

Sticky notes can also be useful for anecdotal records. We like to keep pads of sticky notes in different places in the classroom where we can grab them to jot down something we have noticed or need to do. We can stick the note on our desk and transfer the information later or follow through as appropriate. Because kindergarten classrooms are such busy places, it has been our experience that we'd better write things down quickly or we are likely to forget.

In fact, one year Debra thought she would be looking for a new career. A mom phoned Debra's school to say she would be picking her son up in fifteen minutes for a dentist appointment. The school secretary buzzed into Debra's class to tell her of the early pickup. She was so busy she didn't get to her desk to jot down this message. A little later that day, while Debra was busy in the block area, the boy's mom arrived to take him to the dentist. Not wanting to disrupt the class, Mom slipped into the classroom and quietly guided her son out the door. At the end of the day, while the class was on the playground, Debra called the children to go inside. That is when the problem began. As she counted the children, she realized she was one student short! She looked under and over play equipment but still was one short. She asked her teaching assistant to take the children in and prepare them for dismissal and she stayed outside to continue the search. She was frantic at the thought of losing one of her students. She'd never lost one before!

After the children had been successfully escorted to their buses, Debra ran to her principal and blurted out with terror, "Nancy, please hold the buses. I have lost one of my students!"

Thank goodness for her principal's calmness and administrative experience. She simply said, "Deb, we can hold the buses a few more minutes. Go look some more and get back to me."

Debra thought to herself, "Look some more? I looked everywhere conceivable and I am a complete blank about where to look now."

And that is when Debra's teaching assistant came running out to her, shouting, "Debra, Debra, I just realized Bobby's mom picked him up early. I saw her signature in the office on the sign-out sheet."

Deb thought she would faint with relief. This is why Debra now writes down all messages immediately. There is too much happening in a kindergarten class-room to trust our memories.

Work Samples   Samples of each child's work are another type of formative assessment. We like to create a folder for each student and gather work samples periodically across the subject areas. We try to choose carefully and limit these work samples. If the folder becomes too cumbersome it is not as effective. Monthly samples of each student's writing are especially helpful.

Individual Assessments   The Early Literacy Profile is an assessment used in New York State. Both our districts have modified and adapted this tool for our needs. Some skills we look at to better inform our literacy instruction are letter identification (uppercase and lowercase), letter sounds, sight words, rhyming, letter formation, reading level, and invented spelling. The best way to obtain this information is to sit one-on-one with a child in a relatively quiet setting. This can be very challenging in a busy kindergarten class. Support staff or aides can sometimes help by monitoring your class. In Debra's district each kindergarten teacher has a full-time assistant. This frees the teacher to do these assessments. Bonnie's district provides substitute teachers four days per year to help kindergarten teachers while administering the ELP. We prefer to do the assessments ourselves and let others monitor the rest of the children. We can learn much from the way a child approaches a task and how quickly he performs the task. Often we learn as much by observing the process as we do from the results.

We also assess math and number concepts throughout the year. Most school districts specify the skills to be assessed or use a published program that provides a set of assessments. We have added our own tasks to the assessment to gather additional information we have found helpful.

Social Observations   We also like to know how each child is faring socially. We observe and note whom each child enjoys working and playing with and record comments about the child's interactions with peers in small and large groups. We also ask each child a few questions to learn about her feelings toward school, her peers, and herself. The children feel important when they are interviewed. We ask questions such as Who are your friends? What do you enjoy doing at school? What would you enjoy learning to do better this year? What can you do really well? A child's responses to these questions help us take the child's perspective. If a child sees herself as having no friends, then we can work to change that. It's just another way to get some insights into the child's interests and perceptions of kindergarten.

Summative Assessment

As a teacher learns about each child through formative assessment, it is important to share information with people outside the classroom. Parents at conferences, the child study team, other support teaching staff, and administrators all benefit from summative assessments at some point. Standardized tests are one form of summative assessment, but we are thankful that neither of our school districts requires kindergartners to take any standardized tests. The following are summative assessments that we use.

Progress Reports   Most kindergarten progress reports are a combination of some type of checklist and narrative comments. We think it's important that a progress report be aligned with the goals and philosophies we have for our kindergartners. If the school district does not embrace a common philosophy, this can be difficult. In this case, we recommend using the comment portion to supplement the checklist. Progress report information is primarily intended for the parents, but parents frequently decide to share it with their kindergartners. We include a note with the progress report explaining how the information can be shared in a positive way.

Portfolios   Portfolios are another type of summative assessment. In our districts, we begin a literacy portfolio in kindergarten that will be kept through fifth grade. Debra includes two writing samples from kindergarten and Bonnie is required to gather four writing samples. The information obtained from the ELP is also included in the literacy portfolio. This portfolio goes on to first grade, where teachers continue working with each child, beginning where we left off at the end of kindergarten.

Portfolios can include any number of work samples. We caution teachers that less can be more in this instance. It is our experience that first-grade teachers get to know their children quickly and like to do their own assessments and draw their own conclusions. This is entirely appropriate, since many changes occur in first grade and children can perform very differently. We recommend limiting a portfolio to a few select samples and information that will be valuable to the first-grade teacher. If portfolios become too cumbersome, teachers will not want to sort through the papers to find the most helpful ones. We select a few items we have collected in kindergarten to include in the portfolio for first-grade teachers and send the rest home at the end of kindergarten.

Program Evaluation

Program evaluation means taking a close look at the entire program and reflecting on its effectiveness. This is done in a variety of ways. First, we evaluate our programs continually by self-monitoring the success of individual themes, projects, activities, programs, routines, and even the setup of the classroom. We are always adding, deleting, and refining to better meet the needs of all of the children. Secondly, we are open to suggestions from colleagues, supervisors, and parents. We provide a questionnaire and invite parents to write comments about their children's kindergarten experiences and we read and consider the responses carefully. Our principal also meets with us each year to provide feedback after observing in our classrooms.

Professional Development

We are always on the lookout for opportunities to grow professionally and improve our kindergarten programs. We attend workshops and presentations provided by our school districts and listen to speakers that travel to our area. The children let us know every day if we are doing a good job and where we can do better. We also belong to professional organizations, like our local chapter of the National Association for the Education of Young Children (NAEYC), that offer professional growth opportunities.

Lastly, about a decade ago, we formed a professional growth group with kindergarten teachers from school districts in our area. It originated when Debra facilitated a support group in our capital district sponsored by the local teacher center. The center sent invitations to kindergarten teachers in the area and the response was overwhelming. Clearly, there was a need for kindergarten teachers to get together, exchange ideas, and learn together. This group drew from such a large geographic area and produced such a great number of interested teachers that it was not feasible for it to continue. Instead, teachers were encouraged to form smaller local support groups. Several teachers in our area decided to start a smaller group. It has continued over the years with a group of about eight to ten who still meet regularly. We have met approximately every other month to share the newest children's literature, project ideas, theme materials, and our thinking on current issues and research in our profession. Kindergarten teachers are unique. We have found this group to be supportive and inspiring. We come from different school districts, have a diverse range of experiences, but most importantly, we are passionate about teaching kindergarten. We have continued to meet over the last eleven years to discuss, share, eat, disagree, and laugh about our lives in kindergarten. Over the years, we have become great friends too!

We recommend trying to start a similar group. The teachers union or a regional teacher center or local NAEYC chapter might be a place to recruit interested teachers. We think it is important that teachers in a support group share a similar philosophy. That's not to say there shouldn't be healthy discussions representing different points of view, but if members are too far apart philosophically, it won't be a productive group.

Other professional development opportunities have been organized in collaboration with the local chapter of the NAEYC, the state education department, the teacher center, the Capital Area School Development Organization, and our school districts. We have also helped plan learning opportunities by inviting recognized leaders in early childhood education to work with these professional organizations and our school districts. Some presenters have been Lilian Katz, Leah Mermelstein, Susan Griss, Red Grammer, and Sylvia Chard.

One of the most rewarding and refreshing professional development experiences has been attending a summer retreat held at an elegant old estate in the hills south of Albany. We began the retreat four years ago, staying just one night, and it has now grown to three nights and four days. Debra and Abby Weber, an experienced and inspired kindergarten teacher, organize and lead a variety of workshops for about fifty area kindergarten teachers. As the funding has grown, additional presenters have been invited to share their expertise on kindergarten.

Susan Griss (1998) has presented on ways to address areas of the curriculum through movement. Robert Whiteman, a first-grade teacher who has done extensive work with children's literature, has shared thoughtful information. George Steele, an environmental educator, taught us ways to make connections with nature. And Bonnie and Harriet Fogarty, another member of our kindergarten group, have also shared their expertise over the years.

We also read early childhood journals on a regular basis and some new professional books each year.

We try to make informed choices when selecting workshops and presentations. Time and funds are limited and there are many speakers and workshops available in most places, so we choose reputable presenters. We don't always agree with all they have to say, but we always take some valuable information away. We read, listen to, and learn from many points of view and develop a philosophy to guide the decisions we make. We don't try to implement everything we see and hear at a conference. We integrate ideas and concepts that support our philosophy and guide our teaching. Otherwise we run the risk of presenting children with a collection of cute activities and not a cohesive program. Kindergarten is much more than a series of cute activities and we do ourselves a real injustice if we don't develop a philosophy, clearly state it, and follow it through in our day-to-day work with children, families, and colleagues.

1,000 Book Club Program

The 1,000 Book Club can be a wonderful way to introduce preschoolers to the school and promote literacy development before they even enter kindergarten. Many elementary schools have started a 1,000 Book Club program for preschool children and their families. This book club is a free lending library of new and carefully chosen books. October is a good month to welcome new parents to the program so they can begin reading to their preschoolers. The books are grouped in clusters of ten and are housed in their own numbered canvas bags on a cart.

Ideally, the program has one hundred bags with ten books in each bag. If a family borrows and reads all one hundred bags of books, it will have read one thousand books to their child before he enters kindergarten. It would be difficult to refute the extensive research on the benefits of being read to before entering school. Children who have been read to before entering kindergarten have fewer delays in letter identification, letter-sound correspondence, sight vocabulary, and concepts of print.

Monies for starting such a lending library can be secured through donations from local businesses, small grant programs (Exxon/Mobile, affiliate chapter of NAEYC), PTA contributions, parent donations, and school fund-raisers. It usually takes about a year or two to get the program up and running. It is helpful when a committee of five or more people can work on this so that the startup tasks can be shared.

Once the 1,000 Book Club is up and running, invite the preschool children and families in for a special event with ice cream and a storyteller. While the children are being entertained, teachers can show parents how to use the lending library and assist them in checking out their first book bag.

Figure 3–1. 1,000 Book Club program

Themes, Topics, and Projects

Themes, topics, and projects are defined in many ways by different people. This can get rather confusing, so we will explain how we use the terms. We like Sean Walmsley's definition of a theme as an in-depth exploration of content. Skills can be included but are not the main focus of a theme. He states, "A theme is first and foremost about substantive content (not content areas necessarily, but content), and it digs deep. It never has skills as a primary focus but will emphasize them within the language arts activities during the theme. Different authors use different terms like *theme studies*, *theme units*, or *theme immersions*, but essentially they are referring to themes."

We also agree with Sean's perspective on the difference between topics and themes. He defines a topic as a component of a theme; for example, in a theme on journeys, students and teachers might explore topics such as the migration of animals, space exploration, emigration, and so on. Each of these is a topic within an overall conceptual theme about journeys. However, in the professional literature, there are authors who insist that topics focus on concrete subjects like containers, bats, or ponds, while the term *theme* is reserved exclusively for concepts like flight, interdependence, or survival. We prefer, like Sean, to think that a theme can be about concepts, but it can also explore less abstract ideas like trains, rabbits, and firefighters, so long as its treatment of these topics always allows for engaging children in big ideas.

For example, a theme on bats might be considered just a topic, but if it delves into complex issues like echolocation, the myths surrounding bats, and the role bats play in our ecosystems, then surely this topic is just as conceptual as flight or interdependence. Maybe the moral here is that a theme or topic can't be simply judged by its title. A *theme* on bats that involves children in simply cutting and pasting bat shapes, coloring, or doing cutesy activities is clearly less authentic than a *topic* on bats that engages children in the complexities of echolocation and the role bats play in our ecosystems.

We have worked with Lilian Katz over the years and use her definition of a project. Dr. Katz states, "The key feature of a project is that it is a research effort deliberately focused on finding answers to questions about a topic posed either by students, the teacher, or the teacher working with the students. The goal of a project is to learn more about the topic rather than to seek right answers to questions posed by the teacher."

Themes

Much of the work we do is organized around various themes. Although we are highlighting and describing themes in this chapter, we do themes throughout the year. By using themes we can integrate various subject areas. Themes usually last two or three weeks but we also explore some topics for a shorter period of time and refer to those as minithemes.

Topics for Themes

We find topics to explore in a variety of ways. Some come from holidays and the calendar. In January, as the new year begins, we explore seasons, months of the year, and days of the week. Later that month, we do minithemes as we learn about Martin Luther King Jr. and Chinese New Year. In upstate New York, the seasons produce big changes in nature and we do extensive theme work related to the changes in fall, winter, spring, and summer.

Other sources for themes are topics of interest to kindergartners. Certain topics are inherently interesting to most young children: bats, firefighters, folktales and fairy tales, castles, and giants, to name a few. Additional themes are drawn from required curriculum. Food and nutrition, the life cycle of a chicken, the zoo, and families are examples of topics that may be required by a school district. These are excellent topics for themes.

Topics for themes can also come from the children. Sometimes a class will get excited about a topic after reading a book or having a visitor and will want to learn more. And sometimes we have a passion that we want to share and develop that becomes the basis for a theme. Examples that come to mind are birds, dogs, flowers, famous artists, farm animals, and the life cycle of a monarch butterfly.

Why Themes?

We choose to organize our kindergarten curriculum around themes rather than individual subject areas or a letter of the week because the curriculum can be integrated and taught in a more natural and developmentally appropriate way. For example, during a theme on pumpkins, we transform the dramatic play area into a farm stand where we sell pumpkins, apples, jams, squashes, gourds, berries, pies, and so on. Since this theme would occur in the fall when gardens in our area are ready to be harvested, we bring many of these items to school. When it's not practical to bring the items into the classroom, we improvise. For instance, pies and berries can be created from play dough and jams can made by lining the inside of clear plastic jars with colored paper. We let the children be creative. Their ideas are always better than ours.

Literacy is a big part of any theme and is usually the basis or glue that holds a theme together. Reading to the children provides a wealth of background knowledge, and themes provide genuine topics for children to write about. The following are books we use while doing a theme on pumpkins in kindergarten.

Gibbons, G. 1999. *The Pumpkin Book*. New York: Scholastic.
Hutchings, R., and A. Hutchings. 1994. *Picking Apples and Pumpkins*. New York: Scholastic.
Rockwell, A. 1991. *Apples and Pumpkins*. New York: Scholastic.
———. 1999. *Pumpkin Day, Pumpkin Night*. New York: Scholastic.
Titherington, J. 1989. *Pumpkin Pumpkin*. New York: Scholastic.

When children bring in items that relate to the theme or do simple projects or drawings at home and share them with their friends at school, they are speaking and listening for meaning and understanding. When children draw, paint, and sketch pumpkins, gourds, and apples, they learn other ways to represent their ideas.

Math and science can be taught while counting produce, sorting seeds, weighing and measuring pumpkins, counting money while buying and selling items at the farm stand, and cutting open pumpkins to investigate the gooey insides. This leads to exploring the life cycle of a pumpkin. The life cycle of plants and animals is a concept that recurs many times throughout the kindergarten year, so this is a good time to begin highlighting it. We also do taste test surveys and record the results after asking members of another class to taste products made from pumpkin. Toasted seeds, pumpkin bread, and pumpkin cookies are always favorites for the survey.

All of this learning can be enhanced and extended by a field trip to a pumpkin farm. Good preparation for a field trip is critical to making the most of this educational experience. After all, education is the primary goal of a field trip. We have children brainstorm what they have learned so far and what they would like to learn more about on the trip. We take clipboards and paper to sketch the pumpkins growing in the fields or other aspects of the farm that interest the children. And of course, we bring back produce to enhance our work in the classroom and to cook. We talk more about field trips in the section on projects (page 74).

Music can often be related to the theme as well, but we are careful to choose authentic folk songs and high-quality music or on occasion write our own songs using familiar tunes. We print all our songs on large chart paper so the children are also learning to read as they sing. The children enjoy illustrating the charts. No need to make new ones each year; we just add to our repertoire as we discover new songs.

There are several reasons we like to organize learning around themes.

- It provides us with a way to integrate the curriculum. The curriculum is not fragmented and we make the most of the limited time we have, especially in a half-day kindergarten.
- Themes provide a meaningful goal for literacy activities. Rather than learning skills in isolation, children acquire skills that become a means to an end. Learning about our world is the ultimate goal, not identifying letters and associating sounds with them. Theme teaching shows children the bigger picture and makes learning relevant to their world.
- Themes provide an opportunity to explore a topic more deeply. Themes may last two, three, or even four weeks, depending on the children's interest, the extent of available resources, or how involved we want to get. One thing we have learned over time is less is more. Early in our careers, we tried to teach the children about too many topics rather than take more time to delve deeply into fewer topics. The process is as important as the information students learn. In our world today, we have seemingly limitless information available to us. Children need to learn how to access that information and make sense of it.
- Themes allow children of varying abilities and developmental levels to work together. Rather than sort children by ability and focus solely on skills, we use themes to help children work together and learn from one another.

- Themes also provide a balance of teacher-directed and child-directed activities. We think both are valuable and have their place in the kindergarten classroom.

Where to Begin

When we begin a theme, we gather all the fiction and nonfiction literature that is appropriate and of high quality for kindergartners. We also search for big books, poems, and flannel board materials that relate to the theme. We collect toys, puzzles, games, and math materials that lend themselves to the theme topic. We invite the children to help transform the dramatic play area. We think about different art materials that the children could use and guest speakers we might want to invite that would teach us more about the topic we are exploring.

Next, we put all the theme books in the classroom library and set up a theme center on a table or counter where we place all the related materials for the children to play with and explore. We make these theme centers inviting and attractive. A couple of children make a sign and we hang art the children create there as well as throughout the classroom.

Firefighter's Theme: How Is It Different from a Project?

Another theme we do in October most years is a firefighter's theme. October is Fire Safety Month and the local firefighters visit our classrooms, so we expand on that and develop a theme. In the following section on projects, Debra explains how she explored the topic of fire stations as a project.

The primary differences between a theme on firefighters and a project on firefighters are as follows:

- During a project, the teacher would have a discussion to find out what children already know about firefighters and help them generate questions to be answered. This is optional in a theme.
- A theme does not *require* that children actually visit a fire station and explore the trucks and equipment firsthand. A firefighter may visit your school or a fire truck may even be brought to the school for children to study, sketch, and explore, but this is not required for a theme. A project on a fire station would require that children actually visit the fire station, interview firefighters by asking self-generated questions, and sketch trucks and equipment. This would be considered fieldwork.
- During a theme, children are engaged in activities that integrate the subjects and help them learn more about firefighters and the work they do. The teacher provides extensive literature on the topic in the classroom library

and reads much of it to the children. She may also display items that fire-fighters wear or use. The dramatic play area could be transformed into a fire station or the children may play firefighters outside. Painting, building, drawing, measuring, writing, counting, and playing can all be included during the theme. The difference in a project is that children carry out a variety of investigations and record or represent the results in some way. Building, drawing, writing, surveys, graphs, diagrams, and painting are some ways children can do this.

- One major difference is that a project includes some type of culminating activity to share results. This can mean inviting parents, other classes, other school personnel, or the firefighters to school to see the children's project work. A theme may have some sort of culminating activity, but it is not an integral part of the process.

If you would like to read more about organizing and teaching themes for kindergartners, we recommend *Teaching Kindergarten: A Developmentally Appropriate Approach* (Walmsley, Camp, and Walmsley 1992a). This book explains how to organize and implement a theme-based, developmentally appropriate kindergarten. *Teaching Kindergarten: A Theme-Centered Curriculum* (Walmsley, Camp, and Walmsley 1992b) is a yearlong curriculum binder that outlines a collection of themes with day-by-day instructions on how to implement the themes. *Children Exploring Their World* (Walmsley 1994) explains how children can learn about the world through theme work and provides background on themes.

Project Work

A project is an in-depth investigation of a topic that is worthy of study. The project topic allows the children to pose questions and to uncover answers and information about the topic. Topics should be carefully selected by the class and the teacher. Good topics afford direct observation and study through guest experts, field visits, interviewing, sketching, surveying, and photographing.

Another feature of project study is the length and depth of the topic. That is determined by the resources available, the interest of the children and teachers, and the ability to organize trips and visiting experts that allow the children to uncover information and represent their findings. Therefore, the time period for project study is flexible and not determined precisely at the start.

Project work can strengthen children's disposition to inquire, seek answers, strive for understanding, apply skills in meaningful ways, and work collaboratively with peers in large and small groups.

We began learning about project work many years ago after reading *Engaging Children's Minds: The Project Approach,* by Lilian Katz and Sylvia Chard (1997). Many teachers were interested in learning more, so Debra contacted the authors and arranged to have them work with teachers in our area. Over the course of the last seven years, we have participated in many professional development days on the project approach. Each time, we have studied the project approach in more depth. In addition, some area kindergarten teachers have attended the annual summer institute Engaging Children's Minds at the University of Illinois. Many area kindergarten teachers have collaborated with Lilian Katz and Sylvia Chard at NAEYC annual national conferences. At these sessions, projects from all over the country were shared with attendees. These professional growth opportunities have strengthened our resolve to use project work in our classrooms and have made us more competent and confident.

So what is project work and how does it differ from the wonderful themes many teachers do? We recommend reading *Engaging Children's Minds* as well as *Young Investigators: The Project Approach in the Early Years* (Helm and Katz 2001), *Children Exploring Their World* (Walmsley 1994), and *Project-Based Learning with Young Children* (Diffily and Sassman 2002) as sources for extensive and specific information. Definitions and interpretations of project work vary among different authors. We have based much of what we do on Katz's and Chard's work.

What Is a Project?

A project is the study of a topic that can be investigated firsthand by the children. For example, dinosaurs could be a theme in your classroom but not a project because the children cannot study them directly or call upon people who lived with or knew dinosaurs. On the other hand, topics such as the local supermarket, the fire station, trees outside our windows, and the bakery all make good projects. The children list questions to ask a variety of people related to the topic and visit these sites to seek the answers and obtain more in-depth information. Additionally the children can ask experts such as the store managers, owners, workers, and shoppers to come to class and be interviewed to share more detailed information on the topic.

In-depth projects allow children to formulate their statements of wonder and pose questions (in the beginning, with the teacher's guidance). As our understanding and experience with project work grows, so does our ability to allow project topics to develop with more questions and wonderings from the children.

This is not to suggest that the entire early childhood curriculum should be project work. Since projects can be quite rigorous and go on for three to eight weeks or even longer, most teachers we know do one or two projects each school year.

When we began learning about project work, we were reluctant to attempt a project in the fall. We thought the children were too young, their work skills undeveloped, and their ability to ask good questions and to follow through lacking. So we put off project work to the winter and the spring.

Through experience, reading, reflecting, and actually doing projects in the fall, we have learned that it sets a powerful disposition for inquiry and ownership among the children. A wonderful side effect of project work is ownership. When we are having book discussions, writing meetings, or doing theme work, the children start to ask more questions, begin to design more of their own artwork and buildings, and take more initiative in their learning. This is particularly true for the more capable and mature students, and they become positive models and influences on the rest of the class. This exemplifies the benefits of heterogeneous groupings.

The Fire Station Project

In Debra's class the children had a successful fall project on the topic of the fire station. The class selected this topic as the result of a visiting fire truck and having firefighters visit the school for Fire Safety Week. The specialized equipment on the fire truck such as the jaws of life, dials, pumps, a firefighter's uniform, and the siren fascinated the children. In subsequent days, the students showed lively interest by representing their thinking about what they had seen at the fire station through block building, dramatic play, sketching, and painting. Debra knew this was a worthy topic because the children showed a strong interest and numerous resources were available close to school and within the parent body of the class and school.

Phase One The project was launched a few days after firefighters visited our school. Debra gathered many firefighter props, books, and a complete uniform and put them into a large covered basket. At the meeting she brought out each prop and book one by one, eliciting many oohs and ahhs along with various statements of wonder.

The beginning of project work is called Phase One. In Phase One Debra encouraged the children to "have a go" (in Sylvia Chard's words) in each of the centers during center time. Having a go means trying to represent your ideas and current knowledge on the topic through various materials.

Some children went off and built a fire truck with blocks while others painted fire trucks, ladders, axes, or fire hydrants. The children used a variety of materials including clay, markers, paper, and recycled materials to express their ideas through block building, art, and dramatic play.

After the children had a go for two or three days, they read and discussed nonfiction books about fire stations and fire trucks. Debra asked the children about personal experiences they had related to the topic. A few children told of the time a fire truck came to their neighborhood. Many said they had smoke detectors in their homes and knew about fire hydrants in their neighborhoods. The next day at the class meeting, Debra asked the children what they knew about a fire station, fire trucks, and firefighters and what they wondered more about. This became a springboard to further study. Sylvia Chard summarizes this inquiry process as **E K W Q:**

- children's **E**xperiences with the topic
- what the children **K**now about the topic
- what the children **W**onder about the topic
- what **Q**uestions the children have

While hearing the children's ideas and questions, Debra made a topic web (see Figure 3–2).

Phase Two   A hallmark of project work is to move quickly into fieldwork, which is called Phase Two. Phase Two for this project began with a walking trip to the

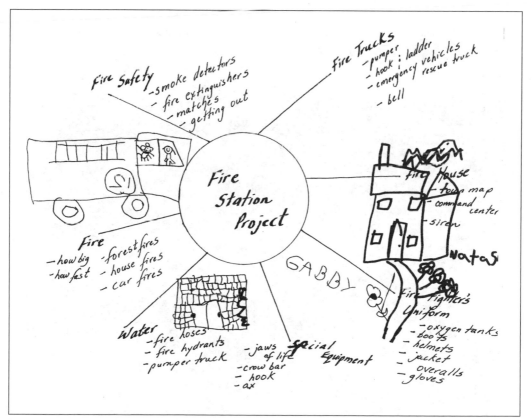

Figure 3–2. Fire station project web

local fire station to gather direct information by observing, questioning, photographing, and sketching. Additionally, two expert firefighting fathers were present to demonstrate their firefighting equipment and answer questions. The firefighters lent Debra's class some authentic firefighting equipment to keep for a few weeks in the classroom. The children used their new knowledge to create a classroom fire station. During this process, they

- created fire trucks and emergency vehicles using giant appliance boxes
- created the command center in the dramatic play area
- used rolls of adding machine paper to measure and to represent the long hose and ladders
- used Popsicle stick bundles in tens and hundreds to show the huge amounts of water in gallons that a pumper truck holds
- used blocks to build a large fire station and firefighting equipment
- worked with assorted craft items such as modeling clay to make fire hydrants, hoses, and ladders

This is a sampling of what the children did as they continued to gain knowledge and get their questions answered. The children added more details as they became *experts* on the topic.

Figure 3–3. Sketching at the fire station

Phase Three   Phase Three of the project is the time to share what the children have documented and learned about the topic. The kindergartners chose to invite their parents and other family guests and their third-grade book buddies to see all they had created in the classroom. The children prepared short statements that described what they had made and the background information they had learned in order to create it. Debra hung photographs with captions around the room that described the three phases and the learning that took place throughout the project.

Scheduling Project Work

This approach to learning requires sustained, uninterrupted work. For this project, Debra chose to do project work every day for a good portion of the day, integrating many curriculum areas. Alternatively she might have scheduled time a few days a week for a specific portion of the day. Most in-depth projects will take about three to six weeks. Project work requires organization, hard work, risk taking, and

Figure 3–4. Measuring the parts of a fire truck with Unifix cubes

it is helpful to have a principal that is knowledgeable or willing to learn about project work. It also requires communication with parents to teach them about the benefits to their children's learning.

As we mentioned earlier, after we became more familiar with project work, we used many of the components in our theme work. Representation, surveys, webs, posing questions, and sharing results are all powerful teaching tools that can be used throughout the school year in all kinds of learning.

Representational Sketching

An important skill we introduce to the children early in the year during theme and project work is representational sketching. Before starting a project or theme, we teach the children to look carefully at items and draw what they see. We can begin in September by sketching a school bus. We encourage them to look at the various shapes of different parts of the bus and add plenty of details. Some children will sit right down with their clipboards and begin to draw, but others will need help to see that the bus is made up of different shapes. By looking carefully at individual parts, they can draw the whole school bus. With this practice and background knowledge of sketching, they are better able to sketch for information during a project or theme.

We have a rule against children shouting out, "I'm done!" while sketching. This usually causes other children to stop sketching prematurely and not produce their best work. The rule is to sketch until sketching time is over. Playing soft classical music in the background is a nice way to help the children focus and take the time to capture as much detail as possible in their sketches.

We ask children to sketch from memory and direct observation. In the beginning of the fire station project, Debra asked her children to sketch a fire truck or any piece of firefighting equipment from memory. She gave each child a three-fold piece of drawing paper on a clipboard (three separate pieces of paper will also work). The children chose to sketch with either a pencil or a black felt-tip marker. The first third of the paper was dated and was the only part of the paper showing.

When Debra's class took a site visit to the fire station, the children took their clipboards. After the children asked their questions, observed, and listened to the firefighters, they each chose a spot on the clean fire station floor to do a second sketch from direct observation. Debra asked them to draw as much detail as possible of some important part of the firehouse. They sketched for about twenty minutes. Most of the children captured much detail in their drawings. When they returned from the fire station, Debra hung these sketches around the room as an excellent source of information for subsequent building and creating in the classroom.

Figure 3–5. Representational sketching of monarch caterpillars

The third sketch on the three-fold paper was done toward the end of the project. Debra asked the children to think about all they had learned and choose something about which they now felt like an expert. She asked them to sketch what they knew a lot about and to use any props, photos, or previous sketches that might help them. This time, after children completed the black-and-white sketches, Debra encouraged them to add appropriate colors. These final sketches clearly stood out as a representation of how much they had learned and now understood about firefighters, fire trucks, and fire stations.

During a theme on firefighters, children used a realistic toy fire truck to sketch in the classroom. The truck had all the gauges, ladders, lights, and other equipment of a real fire truck. Although they did not actually go to the firehouse, they had an opportunity to look carefully and sketch what they saw. This not only improved their sketching skills but made them more observant when looking at fire trucks in the future.

Books for Themes and Projects on Firefighters

Bingham, C. 1995. *Mighty Machines, Fire Trucks and Other Emergency Vehicles.* New York: Dorling Kindersley.

Gibbons, G. 1996. *Emergency!* New York: Scholastic.

Hayward, L. 2001. *A Day in the Life of a Firefighter.* New York: Dorling Kindersley.

Horowitz, J. 1993. *Tonka: Working Hard with the Busy Fire Truck.* New York: Scholastic.

Hutchings, A., and R. Hutchings. 1993. *Firehouse Dog.* New York: Scholastic.

Jeunesse, G., and D. Moignot. 1999. *Fire Fighting: A First Discovery Book.* New York: Scholastic.

Kirkwood, J. 2000. *Cutaway Fire Fighters.* New York: Scholastic.

Kunhardt, E. 1995. *I'm Going to Be a Fire Fighter.* New York: Scholastic.

Maas, R. 1989. *Fire Fighters.* New York: Scholastic.

Rockwell, A. 1986. *Fire Engines.* New York: Puffin.

Simon, S. 2002. *Fighting Fires.* New York: Scholastic.

Summary

October is a full month in kindergarten. With only one major holiday, Columbus Day, we have many days of school this month. By now most of the children have adjusted to their teachers and their peers and know how the classroom works and are capable of more careful schoolwork. During the sustained work of an in-depth theme or project, we are able to make good observational notes that we can use for the children's progress reports and for upcoming parent-teacher conferences.

We have several anecdotal records on each child in various settings and their assessments in language, literacy, and number knowledge. So by the end of October, we have good information about each child's strengths, talents, and areas that need further support or enrichment. In Debra's second year of teaching, she had a few nervous parents who called in early October to say their children were still crying when leaving for school and saying they would rather stay home in the morning. Her wise and experienced principal at that time advised Debra to tell those concerned parents that all would settle in for their children by the end of the month. So before parents become anxious about a shy or reluctant child who has not settled in yet, we encourage them to remain supportive and patient. Children truly do grow at different rates in all areas of their development, and tremendous changes occur by Halloween.

November

A Closer Look

November is a month with fewer days in class. We have days off for parent conferences, Veteran's Day, and Thanksgiving. Generally we do not celebrate holidays in school, but we do recognize and learn about the various cultures that make up our class. Because the spirit of giving thanks is universal and Thanksgiving is part of American history, we share some of our practices at this meaningful time of the year. At the beginning of November, we study the native people that first settled our area, and later in the month, we learn about the Pilgrims coming to Plymouth and the first Thanksgiving.

Native American Theme

We recommend studying the native people that live or lived in your part of the country. Bonnie's school district is called Shenendehowa, which is an American Indian name, and all the school names are American Indian words. The name of her school, Karigon, means "to join together." The Mohawk Indians lived in our area. Almost anywhere we go in this country, there is Native American history. Although kindergartners may not fully understand the concept of time, they can begin to understand that the American Indians were the first people to live where we do now. If there are children of partial Native American background in the class, this theme will be even richer and more meaningful.

   We begin by collecting literature for the theme. We have included a bibliography of the books that we use. They may or may not be appropriate where you live. Let the literature guide you while trying to highlight the main features of the native people that settled your area.

We like to learn about the homes the native people lived in and how they made them, the food they ate and how they got it, the places they traveled and how they got there, the arts and crafts they made and some of the methods and materials they used, the legends that exist, and what they have contributed to our cultures and lives. We try to show the children how the Mohawk Indians made use of the earth's resources and the natural cycles of life to survive in a harsh climate. These are books we have used:

Ashrose, C. 1993. *The Very First Americans*. New York: Grosset and Dunlap.
Black, S. W. 2002. *Let's Read About Squanto*. New York: Scholastic.
Cohen, C. L. 1988. *The Mud Pony*. New York: Scholastic.
dePaola, T. 1989. *The Legend of the Bluebonnet*. New York: Scholastic.
————. 1991. *The Legend of the Indian Paintbrush*. New York: Scholastic.
Jeunesse, G. 1994. *Native Americans: A First Discovery Book*. New York: Scholastic.
McDermott, G. 1977. *Arrow to the Sun: A Pueblo Indian Tale*. New York: Puffin.
————. 1993. *Raven: A Trickster Tale from the Pacific Northwest*. New York: Scholastic.
Reid, M. 1997. *A String of Beads*. New York: Dutton Children's.
Waters, K. 1996. *Tapenum's Day: A Wampanoag Indian Boy in Pilgrim Times*. New York: Scholastic.

We take advantage of our local resources. We have a children's traveling museum that will come to our classroom and present a program titled "They Lived Along the Mohawk." The museum staff brings wonderful authentic artifacts to share and does a presentation about the Mohawk Indians. Each child makes a traditional Mohawk headdress called a *gustoah* and the session ends with a Native American legend.

A book Bonnie has used as the springboard for many Native American activities is *A String of Beads*, written by Margarette S. Reid and illustrated by Ashley Wolff (1997). It is a beautiful introduction to the history of beads and shows how they have been used over the years by different cultures. There is so much information in this book that it can be read to the children in parts or reread several times. We have an extensive collection of beads that the children can examine and explore to see the shapes, colors, and materials they are made from.

The beads can also be used for sorting, which is a math concept taught in kindergarten. There are many ways to sort beads and it is interesting to see what categories the students use. Sorting is an activity best done in a group of six or less.

The children use different colored and shaped beads to copy patterns already printed on cards and then they create their own patterns. The children can count, weigh, balance, and write their names with beads. We encourage the children to bring beaded items to share. One day we all wear beads to school. (We have some extras on hand in case someone forgets.) When we are all wearing our beads, we like to begin the day in the Meeting and Greeting Circle with each person telling about his beads. One year a student strung a bracelet for each child in the class using different colored plastic beads. Each bracelet had a pattern so it was a wonderful math lesson as we each identified our pattern and then identified the patterns on other children's bracelets. A string of one hundred beads using a different color for every ten beads is a great way to illustrate the concept of one hundred and teach counting by tens.

We also make beads from red clay by rolling it into balls and cylinders and poking a hole with a toothpick or nail. The clay we use self-hardens in a few days. After they are dry and hard, we paint the beads and string them.

We know people who make jewelry with beads and ask them to come to talk to the children and we even have a bead shop where we can go on a field trip, or we may invite someone from the shop to visit the class.

There are many different art activities the children can do with a Native American theme. We also use the red clay to make small pots that can be dried and painted or just left natural. There is an episode of the PBS show *Reading Rainbow* in which *The Legend of the Indian Paintbrush*, by Tomie dePaola (1991), is read and then native people are shown making clay pots. Your school media specialist may have a copy or be able to obtain one from your local PBS station. This is an excellent introduction for making our own clay pots.

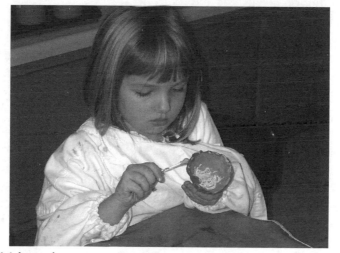

Figure 4–1. Making clay pots

Figure 4–2. Picture writing on "deerskin"

There are many topics for writing. The wonderful legends inspire children to draw and write. We write about American Indians that lived in our area and create a class nonfiction collaborative book.

One traditional Native American chant that our children love is called "Return." It can be found on a series of CDs that are produced by Heinemann and performed by Mary Alice Amidon. They are sold in conjunction with *Teaching Kindergarten: A Theme-Centered Curriculum* (Walmsley, Camp, and Walmsley 1992b) or can be purchased separately.

We teach the children to do picture writing using symbols to tell a story. By taking a paper bag, crumpling it all up and then flattening it and tearing the corners, we make "deerskin." The children write their picture stories on the deerskin.

Pilgrims

As we approach Thanksgiving, we read *Let's Read About Squanto*, by Sonia W. Black (2002). Squanto was an American Indian that helped the Pilgrims. This book makes a good transition to a study of the Pilgrims and discussions of being thankful. The Pilgrims were grateful for all Squanto did to help them and as the harvest was brought in, the Pilgrims wanted to give thanks. This topic can produce some interesting discussions about settlers taking the natives' land and treating them badly. Kindergartners don't shy away from questions. They are very curious and get to the point. We try to bring these discussions to their level by relating issues to our classrooms or their families.

A great book to share with kindergartners about the Pilgrims is National Geographic Society's *Pilgrims of Plymouth* (2001). This book has minimal text with brilliant color photographs that were taken at Plimoth Plantation, a replica village. Again, we bring the concept of giving thanks to the children's lives. We read, draw, and write about what we have to be thankful for and often create something for the Thanksgiving table. We sing a song called "Thanks a Lot" that can also be found on the CDs that were produced for *Teaching Kindergarten: A Theme-Centered Curriculum*. Kindergartners tend to be egocentric, so don't be too discouraged if they tell you they are thankful for their bikes or video games. And pets often rate higher than family members when kindergartners give thanks!

A colleague at Debra's school made a multimedia program one year in early November. Robert Whiteman and his wife, Beth, took a trip to the historic village of Plimoth Plantation in Plymouth, Massachusetts. With permission, they photographed the village and costumed guides. Through the use of computer software, they created an interactive program through which children could view authentic information about native people, Pilgrims, and life four hundred years ago. The program had many links that could be opened to get more in-depth information on specific parts of the village. The video was posted on the school district's website and all teachers and students had access to it. Even now, a few years after the Whitemans made the original video, children tell Robert how they loved the show and watched it again and again in their class. It continues to be a rich resource when teaching about Thanksgiving. This is one of those great ways to use technology with young children in the classroom.

Books About Thanksgiving

Gibbons, G. 1983. *Thanksgiving Day*. New York: Holiday House.

Goodman, S. E. 2001. *Pilgrims of Plymouth*. Washington, DC: National Geographic Society.

Melmed, L. K. 2001. *This First Thanksgiving Day: A Counting Story*. New York: Scholastic.

Raphael, E., and D. Bolognese. 1991. *The Story of the First Thanksgiving*. New York: Scholastic.

Ross, K. 1995. *The Story of the Pilgrims*. New York: Random House.

Shuter, J., and F. Reynoldson. 1991. *Thanksgiving*. Crystal Lake, IL: Rigby.

Writing Revisited

Later in the fall and in early winter, it is appropriate to start looking for more details in the stories the children write. We also find the children can write more than one page to tell their stories. Typically each page has an illustration and corresponding words or a sentence.

The things we share in our mini writing lessons and the features of books we use to show the children important things about stories and authors will affect the children's writing throughout the year. We read several books that become touchstone texts that we use repeatedly to illustrate a point we want to make about writing.

Touchstone texts result from thoughtfully and purposefully reading certain books in our writing minilessons. There is really no way to designate a book as a

Figure 4–3. Winter writing samples show more sound-spelling attempts, more details in illustrations, and longer stories: —"My dog died long ago," "Bruno" (dog's name), by Sophie.

touchstone text before we have used it for a while with the children. Touchstone texts illustrate techniques author use.

Books We Have Used as Touchstone Texts

Asch, F. 1994. *The Earth and I.* New York: Harcourt Brace.

Brown, M. W. 1977. *The Important Book.* New York: Harper Collins.

Crews, D. 1978. *Freight Train.* Big book. New York: Greenwillow.

Ehlert, L. 1990. *Feathers for Lunch.* New York. Trumpet Club.

Fox, M. 1994. *Sophie.* New York: Harcourt Brace.

———. 1996. *Tough Boris.* New York: Trumpet Club.

Greenfield, E. 1972. *Honey, I Love.* New York: Viking.

London, J. 2000. *What Do You Love?* Orlando, FL: Harcourt.

Shannon, D. 1998. *No, David!* New York: Blue Sky.

———. 1999. *David Goes to School.* New York: Blue Sky.

———. 2002. *David Gets in Trouble.* New York: Blue Sky.

Whitehouse, P. 2002. *Plant ABC.* Chicago: Heinemann.

Wood, A. 1994. *Quick as a Cricket.* New York: Scholastic.

Parent-Teacher Conferences

In our school districts, November is the month to hold our first parent-teacher conferences. Debra's district holds conferences in the fall and the spring. Although it is difficult to be out of the classroom to meet with parents twice a year, we think it is worthwhile. In the fall, the teachers have a lot to learn from the parents, and in the spring, we have more to share about the children with parents. At Open House in late September, parents choose a convenient time for their November conferences. We send confirmation notices in mid-October.

Teachers with two half-day sessions will have as many as fifty conferences depending upon their class sizes. Needless to say, organization is key when conducting this number of effective and informative conferences.

Some schools close and keep students home for two days while teachers hold conferences and some schools provide substitutes for whole or half days so teachers can complete conferences. It is easier when the children are not in the classroom simply because the conferences can be held there and parents get a better feel for the classroom environment, and anything you want to show parents is handy. Twenty-five-minute time slots work well with occasional short breaks that help prevent delays. We also leave a few minutes between conferences to write our thoughts and parents' comments. If you know in advance that a conference will need more time, it is helpful to plan for it. Conferences can be exhausting, so we set things up to minimize the stress.

When teaching two half-day sessions, teachers may want to have a photo of each child at the conference and color-code things for A.M. and P.M. classes. Although teachers know the children quite well by this time, with so many students, it can be difficult to remember if a child is A.M. or P.M.

Once the schedule is worked out, we are ready to begin conferences. We have sent a questionnaire home to parents prior to this conference. It asks questions about the growth and development of each child. It is a wonderful basis for beginning the conference. We ask parents to return the form a week before their conference so that we have time to read it and make any notes.

During the weeks leading up to the conferences, we hold a brief interview with each child, asking her about her friends and feelings. This gives us each child's perspective on his or her kindergarten experience.

This is how we organize our conferences:

- warm welcome to the parents
- greeting and a bit of general talk
- discuss parent questionnaire
- discuss fall assessment pieces
- share the interview we had with the child
- show some work samples and first writing pieces
- discuss work during centers (small-group instruction)
- ask parents if they have any questions or concerns that haven't been addressed

If a child is weak at letter and number identification, we want to give parents some ideas and developmentally appropriate materials to help boost these skills. In Debra's school a small reading book on best practices is given to every parent. A kindergarten workbook is offered to the parents of children who need a bit more letter reinforcement. If the parents are receptive to doing some work at home, then the teacher and parents work out a plan. For children who are the most delayed academically, little kits with markers, paper, glue sticks, scissors, and so on can be given to the parents for home use. Parents are quite pleased to be provided with some specific ways to help their children. We encourage parents to have their children bring to school any finished pages or activities that they would like us to see.

We use the spring conference mainly to explain the progress a child has made. If a child is not developing normally, we need to provide work samples and specific examples to illustrate our points. It is also helpful to have a plan ready to propose to the parents. If a child is truly struggling, we have been in contact with those parents throughout the school year. We know the importance of good communication. Conferences are one way we can communicate. Although we have only one or two scheduled conferences in the school year, we are always willing to meet with, phone, email, or jot a note to parents whenever a need arises.

Summary

Although November is shorter in terms of teaching days, it is a rich month filled with Native American and Pilgrim history. In recent years, some very good nonfiction books have been published to teach young children about Native Americans, Pilgrims, and the first Thanksgiving. The children have matured and better understand the difference between fact and fantasy and are very curious about our American history. They are writing more and their drawings show significant improvement. They take more care with their work and are proud of the results. We sense they are excited by the content of the themes and projects and are eager to learn more. As one theme draws to a close, they are already asking what we will learn about next.

We have now met with all the parents and feel a bit of relief about having all the conferences behind us. We also feel as though we know the children better and have gained insights and understanding about the children from their parents. We have definitely bonded with this year's students and think about them long after we have left the classroom.

December
A Time to Celebrate

December can be an exciting and hectic month in kindergarten. On the first day of December, children who celebrate Christmas are already feeling the excitement. It doesn't help that the stores have been displaying Christmas merchandise since the day after Halloween, the holiday specials are aired weeks before the holidays arrive, and many families put up their Christmas trees the day after Thanksgiving. December can be a challenging month in kindergarten.

Holidays and customs vary greatly among families and schools. We do not celebrate any of the December holidays but instead learn about the customs, holidays, and traditions of the cultures that our class represents. This is a natural way to understand and respect the diversity in the classroom. We believe it is difficult for five-year-olds to relate to all the holidays that could be celebrated in December. Instead we let the population in our class determine which holidays to explore.

Holidays

Over the years we have invited parents to class to talk to us about holidays they celebrate. We find it helpful to set up a schedule two or three weeks in advance. This way parents get plenty of notice at a busy time of year. Even if the majority of our class celebrates Christmas, there is diversity among families as to how they celebrate Christmas at their homes or with their extended families. Some of the things we suggest parents do to share their holiday customs are

- read a story
- cook or bake a family recipe in the classroom
- play a game
- make a craft

- share photos
- bring artifacts to class from their homes and discuss their significance (e.g., a menorah or an Advent wreath)

Holiday Books

Brett, J. 1994. *Christmas Trolls*. New York: Scholastic.
Brown, M. 1984. *Arthur's Christmas*. Boston: Little, Brown.
Say, A. 1991. *Tree of Cranes*. New York: Scholastic.
Van Allsburg, C. 1985. *The Polar Express*. Boston: Houghton Mifflin.

Minithemes

Another option for December can be theme work. Numbers, gingerbread men, and trains are all themes we have done successfully during December. Usually we devote a few days or a week to each of these themes, so we refer to them as minithemes.

Holiday Counting

During a theme on numbers, we planted paperwhite (narcissus) bulbs on marble chips. We gave each child a ten-box grid and asked him to count out one hundred marble chips by placing ten chips in each box. The marble chips can be purchased

Figure 5–1. Paperwhites grow on the windowsill.

at garden supply stores. Paperwhite bulbs are great to use because they grow so quickly and produce beautiful white flowers that are very fragrant. The children are always amazed and very proud of them when they take them home to share with their families at the holidays.

Another way we have expanded on the number theme at this time of year is by bringing a large bag of potatoes to school. We estimate, count, and weigh them before using some to make latkes. We talk to the children about the history of Hanukkah and the significance of making latkes. We have also taught the children the counting rhyme "One Potato, Two Potatoes" and had each child illustrate a small book with the rhyme printed in it. They illustrate the books by drawing the accurate number of potatoes on each page and can then read the books and play the game with their families.

Gingerbread Men

Baking gingerbread men and making gingerbread houses are traditions for many families at this holiday time. Children enjoy hearing several versions of the gingerbread man story and doing related activities. Following are the versions that we have read to our kindergartners:

Aylesworth, J. 1998. *The Gingerbread Man*. New York: Scholastic.
Bell, S. 1990. *The Gingerbread Man*. New York: Golden.
Brett, J. 2000. *Gingerbread Baby*. New York: Scholastic.
Egielski, R. 1997. *The Gingerbread Boy*. New York: Harper Collins.
Galdone, P. 1975. *The Gingerbread Boy*. New York: Houghton Mifflin.
McCloskey, R. 1978. *Journey Cake, Ho!* New York: Puffin.
Parkes, B., and J. Smith 1987. *The Gingerbread Man*. *Big book*. Crystal Lake, IL: Rigby.
Schmidt, K. 1967. *The Gingerbread Man*. New York: Scholastic.

We have extended these books and integrated other subject areas in a number of ways, such as

- making masks and simple costumes and dramatizing different versions of the story
- using flannel boards to retell the story
- making charts to compare different versions
- drawing story maps to retell the story with illustrations
- making large wall stories for which each child draws a part of the story with a partner and writes text beneath the drawing to retell a version of the story
- baking and decorating gingerbread people
- using fun foam, buttons, and puff paint to make gingerbread men

Figure 5–2. Dramatizing "The Gingerbread Man"

As a remembrance of kindergarten, Bonnie uses polymer clay and a small cookie cutter to make each child a special gingerbread figure. She adds eyes and buttons with seed beads and makes a hole to hang it with a ribbon. It makes a good gift for all children at this time of year.

Trains

Many of us have childhood memories of trains at this time of year. Bonnie often does a theme on trains in December. Her father worked for the railroad and she has fond memories of taking trains as a child and still loves riding trains today. It is fun to set up different trains in the classroom such as wooden Brio sets and plastic trains, and sometimes a parent will even bring an electric one to school. Bonnie has found that the children are thrilled to assemble the wooden tracks in various configurations and push the little trains on the tracks. Many young children today don't have enough imaginative play with toys that are not battery-operated or electronic.

Bonnie may have a conductor or engineer visit her classroom and talk to the children. If Bonnie's school were close enough to a train station, she would take a field trip. This theme lends itself to some wonderful block building and dramatic play as well as interesting art projects and representations. There is great literature on this topic as well. *Freight Train*, by Donald Crews (1978), teaches children the different cars on a freight train. Gail Gibbons also has a good book on trains.

Train Books

Crebbin, J. 1997. *The Train Ride*. Cambridge, MA: Candlewick.

Crews, D. 1978. *Freight Train*. New York: Puffin.

Gibbons, G. 1998. *Trains*. New York: Scholastic.

Hillenbrand, W. 2000. *Down by the Station*. New York: Scholastic.

Jeunesse, G. 1998. *Trains: A First Discovery Book*. New York: Scholastic.

Lewis, K. 2000. *Chugga-Chugga Choo-Choo*. New York: Scholastic.

Magee, D., and R. Newman. 1990. *All Aboard ABC*. New York: Dutton.

Neitzel, S. 2000. *I'm Taking a Trip on My Train*. New York: Scholastic.

Quattlebaum, M. 1999. *Underground Train*. New York: Random House.

Rockwell, A. 1988. *Trains*. New York: Puffin.

Siebert, D. 1991. *Train Song* (with audiotape). New York: Trumpet Club.

Westcott, N. 1996. *I've Been Working on the Railroad*. New York: Trumpet Club.

Winterfest

A wonderful tradition that started many years ago at Debra's school is the annual Winterfest. This celebration includes all the children and families in the primary (K–2) wing. The Winterfest replaces traditional holiday parties. Because of our students' diverse backgrounds and heightened sensitivity to this diversity, it is no longer appropriate to do what we did in the past. This new tradition allows everyone to come together at this happy and exciting time of year and it builds community in the school. The Winterfest is held during a school day for approximately two hours. Usually the event is held on the last Friday before the winter break. Each kindergarten, first-grade, and second-grade teacher in the primary wing chooses an activity or craft to offer the day of the festival. Each child is accompanied by a parent, relative, or book buddy as he participates in the crafts and activities. Some examples are

- picture frames
- origami peace doves to string or hang alone
- bird feeders from stuffed pine cones
- strings of cranberries and popcorn
- sand jars
- felt door knob panels

Figure 5–3. Winterfest craft choices

- wrapping paper
- miniature evergreen wreaths

One teacher agrees to host the Winterfest café. That teacher is responsible for setting up the refreshments and seeing that all goes smoothly during the festival. The café job is rotated each year. It is a big undertaking, but it is wonderful to get to talk to so many current and former families as they stop by for refreshments.

Author Studies

We like to regularly highlight an author in our classroom libraries. We collect their books, display photographs, and collect jacket covers. Sometimes we have posters that we add to the displays. Using these items, we design an attractive and informative bulletin board to complement the books. We place the books on a display stand so the front covers are visible and inviting.

If the author also illustrates her work, we draw the children's attention to the artwork and talk about how the illustrations were made (e.g., watercolors, clay, collage). As we learn more about the author-illustrator, we may ask the children to reproduce that style of artwork. There are videos available about most authors and illustrators that allow children to "meet" the authors and learn about their

Figure 5–4. Lois Ehlert books on display for an author study

lives and how they create their books. We use one about Lois Ehlert titled *Color World* (produced by the Trumpet Club) that truly inspires the children and their teachers. There is also a wonderful video about Eric Carle titled *Story Writer*. We have used this toward the end of the year. It tends to be long for kindergartners, so we recommend either showing part of it or watching it in two or three sessions. We have also used videos about Marc Brown and Mem Fox. As always, we preview the video and decide in advance how to use it with our students.

As we become familiar with different authors and author-illustrators, we find that many lend themselves to particular themes or seasons of the year. For example, many of Jan Brett's stories occur in the winter, so we tend to highlight her work in December or January. Spot books by Eric Hill are interactive and appropriate for younger children, so putting his books in the class library for the opening of school works well. The children are often familiar with his work and it can be comforting to see their friend Spot in the library as they enter kindergarten for the first time.

We are partial to Marc Brown's work. Marc is Bonnie's brother. (And she is the inspiration for Francine.) Often we will highlight the D. W. books early in the year because they are written for a younger audience. We save the Arthur books and Marc's other work for May. They have more text and more sophisticated story lines. Bonnie and her husband, Sean Walmsley, have written a book for Scholastic called *Teaching with Favorite Marc Brown Books* (1998). This book gives inside information about Marc (as only a sister could do) and loads of ideas on using his books in the classroom.

There are several authors and author-illustrators that we think work well for author studies in kindergarten: Eric Hill, Mercer Mayer, Tomie dePaola, Jan Brett, Lois Ehlert, Eric Carle, Rosemary Wells, Frank Asch, Paula Bourgeois, Donald Crews, Mem Fox, Dr. Seuss, and Marc Brown.

Jan Brett Author Study

As we mentioned, Jan Brett's work lends itself to a successful December author study. Many of her books take place in a setting of snow and cold similar to our winter holidays. Her books frequently have a main character who overcomes adversity and resolves a conflict. This aspect of her work lends itself to discussions and book extensions. Jan Brett's illustrations are remarkable and give the children great models for drawing in their own books. These are some of the Jan Brett books we use:

Brett, J. 1985. *Annie and the Wild Animals*. Boston: Houghton Mifflin.
———. 1989. *The Mitten*. New York: Scholastic.
———. 1992. *Trouble with Trolls*. New York: Puffin.
———. 1993. *Christmas Trolls*. New York. G. P. Putnam's Sons.
———. 1996. *Comet's Nine Lives*. New York: Scholastic.
———. 1997. *The Hat*. New York: G. P. Putnam's Sons.
———. 2000a. *Gingerbread Baby*. New York: Scholastic.
———. 2000b. *Hedgie's Surprise*. New York: Scholastic.
———. 2002. *Who's That Knocking on Christmas Eve?* New York: G. P. Putnam's Sons.

A favorite and one that lends itself beautifully to a collaborative class book extension is *Trouble with Trolls*. When working on this book extension, we guide the children to emulate Jan Brett's style by adding elaborate detail and many colors.

A manageable way we have found for the children to illustrate their pages is to focus on one aspect per day.

- Each child creates a border around the perimeter based on something that will be in her illustration.
- The child draws the illustration that shows the action.
- The child writes the words that describe the illustration.

We complete the book by having a small group make a cover, having each child sign the author-illustrator page, and adding a final parent comment page.

Figure 5–5. Owen's page from a class book extension, "Trouble with Trolls in Our Classroom." He wrote, "Owen gave away the blocks."

These book extensions are another meaningful writing opportunity for the children.

Jan Brett has many more titles; for a complete list and other wonderful classroom resources, log onto her website at *www.JanBrett.com*. There is a good chance Jan Brett will write back to your class if you write to her. Over the years we have received some exciting mail from her. It delights the children to get a response and an autographed poster or picture as well.

Summary

December can be quite hectic. Not only are there special things we want to do with the children in class, but many extra projects await us at home. In December, we try to keep all the classroom activities and plans relaxed. We avoid adding any stress to the children's lives. Why would we add to the feverish pitch of excitement and anticipation as we approach Christmas and the other December holidays?

By learning about each other's customs and traditions, we better blend the world of home and school. The children now know their teacher and classmates very well. It is an appropriate time for them to share their families' customs. We have found our children are so proud and animated when their parents comes to school to talk about their holidays and ways of celebrating. The children are not the only ones to learn and feel enriched. As teachers, we have grown in our understanding and appreciation of other family holidays and traditions and it has been a joy to get to know our families in this way.

From the start of the school year we have worked hard to create a community of caring learners. It is now appropriate to branch out a bit and join with other classes in an activity such as the Winterfest to extend that caring community. On Winterfest day the school feels especially warm, welcoming, and happy. What a splendid way to say good-bye to the old year and to wish everyone the happiest of holidays. On the last school day before the holiday break, a piano is rolled to the front entryway of Debra's school and the faculty and staff sing to each class as they go by to board the buses. We continue to wave and sing as the last bus pulls away. We hope to build stronger and more caring bonds as we celebrate and enjoy these special times together.

January

New Year, New Horizons

By January the children have become far more independent and we are getting a clearer picture of their development. The child who has difficulty listening to stories, taking turns, playing cooperatively, or identifying most of the letter names and numbers to twenty is the exception. The start of a new calendar year is a logical time to focus on the months of the year and the days of the week.

Raising the Bar

January is also a time to hone skills like name writing, letter and number formation, and identification of numbers from ten to thirty and for some children even higher. Many children are beginning to associate sounds with letters. This growth is reflected in their writing. The children are bigger, stronger, more mature, and generally comfortable with their peers and surroundings. It is appropriate to have higher expectations for their work and responsibilities.

We sneak a good deal of academic work into our coming-in time now. This is the time when the children enter the classroom at the start of each day. We may ask them to write their names (including last names now), phone numbers, or street addresses as they enter the classroom. We might start having a word of the day and ask them to read a word found in a pocket chart near the door as they arrive. We select these words from a list of sight words that our students are expected to read by the end of kindergarten or early first grade.

Kindergarten is the beginning of formal literacy instruction, but we are careful not to push down the first-grade curriculum to kindergarten. Even though our students present a wide range of developmental levels, there is an expectation that kindergartners will acquire certain skills. We know where our children are in their development and try to move them forward all year. Many children exceed the benchmark standards for a kindergartner. Others end the year just about on schedule, and some may enter first grade before they have met the expectations for a kindergartner. And on rare occasions, after thorough review and consultation, we may have a child spend an additional year in kindergarten.

Much of our literacy instruction is woven into themes, projects, morning meeting, and coming-in time. We also work in small groups for writing and read individually with the children. Many states have set the standards higher for all children. We feel it is possible to meet these standards and get children off to a strong start in their literacy development without compromising our philosophy of a developmentally appropriate kindergarten.

Evaluation

This is a good time of year to revisit the assessment plan. We send home progress reports in February or March, so this gives us time to gather information and prepare the reports.

We do not reassess previously mastered skills unless a child was very uncertain about them. We simply continue where we left off in October. By using a different color of ink for each assessment period, we can look back and determine when the skills were acquired. We usually begin by asking the child to identify letters that could not be identified previously and move through other items on the Early Literacy Profile and the math checklist. Since we are experienced, it has become second nature to skip certain skills that are beyond a child and try them at a later date. We are mindful not to frustrate a child by asking him too many items in one session or asking items that are too advanced. Depending on the child, the assessment may need to be done in several sittings. We have learned it is important not to do too much at once or we will not get the child's best effort. More students are ready for a running record in January. We try to allow enough time for this and although the children may be at very early reading levels, it gives us a good baseline.

After collecting all the information and reviewing anecdotal records and recent work samples, it is time to begin the progress reports. We do these at home on our computers, where we can really spread things out and work at all times of the day or night. By this time of the year, we know the children very well and if progress is still slow with particular children, it is time to intervene. For some children the delay has been significant so we have taken advantage of services available to help at-risk students. Other children just needed time to settle in and get some good instruction, and by now they are developing normally. We will carefully consider the needs of children who are still struggling to learn basic skills and concepts.

We find it is best to talk to the parents before sending home a progress report indicating that the child is not developing in the normal range. We expressed some concerns at the fall conference, but it is time to do so again. Parents assume no news is good news, so we communicate concerns regularly. If parents do not attend the conference and do not respond to notes or phone calls we feel it is still our responsibility to inform them. We offer to visit the home (perhaps with a counselor). We discuss this with our principal first to determine if this is appropriate. Or we send a letter in the mail sharing our concerns. Children who struggle in school frequently have parents who struggled in school. Those parents may have had a poor school experience themselves and are uncomfortable coming to the school and talking with teachers. They may be overwhelmed with their day-to-day routines. We try not to let our frustrations with a parent get in the way of doing our very best for the child.

Borrowing Books

We both have a system for loaning leveled books to the children. The mechanics may vary but the outcome is the same. We organize our books by level of difficulty in baskets and boxes. There are many publishing companies that produce leveled books. Some of the ones we have used are Wright Group, Rigby, Sundance, and Scholastic. We begin loaning these books once a week in January. During her center time, Bonnie calls children up individually and gives them two books from their reading level each week. Most children start with the very first level. Bonnie will usually select one book and have the child select one. She sends the books home in an eleven-by-fourteen-inch envelope. She records the books that have been loaned on the outside of the envelope. When the student returns the books the following week, Bonnie simply crosses the titles off the outside of the envelope and the child gets two more books to bring home. Bonnie takes time to listen to each child read as she swaps the books. This way she tracks the children's growth and knows when they are ready to move to a higher level. She also sends home a letter explaining to the parents the best way to use these books. Parents also have a record sheet so they can respond and provide feedback to the teacher. Most children love these books and it becomes an exciting event to get their new books each week. Since the books are patterned, predictable, and highly dependent on picture clues at the early levels, the children can be successful immediately.

In Debra's room the children can borrow new books as they return ones they've read. Children read to the teacher or the assistant when they bring back their books. Debra has a full-time teaching assistant so she can be available to read daily with her students when they return their books. She records each title in

Figure 6–1. A child reads her borrowed book.

a simple folder and makes brief notes about the child's reading that day. Over time this is a strong record of each child's beginning reading development.

Months of the Year and Days of the Week Theme

As we head back to school in the new year, it is a good time to do a short theme on the months of the year and the days of the week. The months can be taught while focusing on birthday months. We have been celebrating each child's birthday until now but we have not emphasized learning the names of the months and understanding when they occur throughout the year. Very few things are more important to five-year-olds than their birthdays and there is plenty of good literature to read about birthdays. *Night Noises*, by Mem Fox (1989), and *Arthur's Birthday*, by Marc Brown (1989), are two we often read. Greg and Steve have a song about the months (sung in English and Spanish) on their CD *We All Live Together, Volume 2* (1978). And Mary Alice Amidon has a great song for the months of the year on one of the CDs that accompany *Teaching Kindergarten: A Theme-Centered Curriculum* (Walmsley, Camp, and Walmsley

Figure 6–2. Birthday Graph

1992b). Jean Feldman has "Macarena Months" and "Days of the Week" on her CD *Dr. Jean and Friends* (1998). Another great song for the days of the week is "Today Is Monday." It is based on the book illustrated by Eric Carle (1993). Scholastic has produced an audio tape including the song called *The All-Year-Long Songbook* (1987).

An old favorite book that includes a short poem about each month is *Chicken Soup with Rice*, by Maurice Sendak (1962). It is also available as a big book and in song. We sing the song version of *Chicken Soup with Rice*, which is performed by Carole King. Singing is a powerful way to help children learn the months.

We make a large birthday graph using a digital photo of each child that has been mounted and laminated with her name under her photo.

It is helpful to use their birthday months as a transition. For example, "Everyone with a birthday in February can line up, then September, then March. . . ." We ask each child to do a painting of his birthday celebration. Associating months with birthdays and other holidays and celebrations helps the children remember them and attach meaning to an abstract concept.

When teaching about the months, we also relate them to the seasons. We drew four maple trees and discussed how the trees might look during the different seasons and wrote the season near each tree. We have also collected several pictures depicting activities typical of all four seasons and laminated them to use for sorting. After doing this together, the children can revisit this activity independently or in pairs. We write the correct season on the back, which helps the children check for accuracy without an adult.

In January, the children make their own calendars by writing numbers on blank calendars. This activity can be modified by printing some numbers on the calendar in advance and letting the children complete the blank spaces. We even ask parents to collect extra calendars and pick up free ones and send them to school so we can let each child select one. The children can personalize them by drawing icons for family birthdays and holidays. Having their own calendars to take home piques their interest about the months and the days.

Books About Months and Days

Carle, E. 1969. *The Hungry Caterpillar*. New York: Philomel.

———. 1993. *Today Is Monday*. New York: Scholastic.

Carlstrom, N. W. 1999. *How Do You Say It Today Jesse Bear?* New York: Aladdin Paperbacks.

dePaola, T. 1988. *Cookie's Week*. New York: Putnam and Grosset.

Florian, D. 1989. *A Year in the Country*. New York: Greenwillow.

Hill, E. 1983. *Spot's Busy Year*. New York: G. P. Putnam's Sons.

Min, L. 1994. *Mrs. Sato's Hens*. Glenview, IL: Scott Foresman.

Sendak, M. 1962. *Chicken Soup with Rice*. New York: Scholastic.

Birthday Books

Brown, M. 1989. *Arthur's Birthday*. New York: Trumpet Club.

Fox, M. 1989. *Night Noises*. New York: Trumpet Club.

Frasier, D. 1991. *On the Day You Were Born*. Orlando: Harcourt Children's Books.

Hoban, R. 1968. *A Birthday for Frances*. New York: Scholastic.

Holabird, K. 1989. *Angelina's Birthday Surprise*. New York: Trumpet Club.

Martin Luther King Jr.

Children are intrigued by Martin Luther King Jr. and the principles he believed in and how he promoted justice for all people in a peaceful manner. We usually begin the discussion by showing the children a photo of King and asking the children if they know this man. The responses vary from Michael Jordan to Marc Brown. We read several books throughout the month about King that produce thoughtful and serious discussions. One that is well written for kindergartners is *Happy Birthday, Martin Luther King* (1993), by Jean Marzolla. Another book with beautiful illustrations is *Martin's Big Words* (2001), by Diane Rappaport. We have found that the text in this book is too extensive for kindergartners, so we either paraphrase and show the pictures or read only the text in larger print. We learn a great song titled "I Just Want to Sing Your Name" that is on one of the CDs that accompany *Teaching Kindergarten: A Theme-Centered Curriculum*. It is an easy song for kindergartners because they simply echo Mary Alice Amidon as she sings and plays the banjo. Children often refer to Martin Luther King Jr. long after we have celebrated his birthday. We can draw many parallels as we strive to create a caring, fair, and peaceful community in kindergarten.

Chinese New Year

This holiday is another opportunity to teach children about customs and celebrations in other cultures. If we have a family that celebrates Chinese New Year and they are willing to come to school, we prefer to do that. Many families have taught us about their customs and shared food at this exciting time of year. If we don't have someone who can visit our classroom, we read a book called *Lion Dancer, Ernie Wan's Chinese New Year* (1990), by Kate Waters and Madeline Slovenz-Low. This is the story of a young boy who is preparing to do his first lion dance in the streets of Chinatown in New York. The book describes the traditions and customs in Ernie's family for Chinese New Year. Another wonderful story is *Sam and the Lucky Money* (1997), by Karen Chinn and Cornelius Van Wright. This is a moving story of a boy who receives four dollars in four red envelopes as part of the traditional Chinese New Year celebration and soon discovers the value of money and decides to give his money to a homeless man instead of buying candy or a toy for himself.

Over the years we have collected many items like cards, prints, tapestries, menus, and red envelopes to show the children. We even try to write some Chinese characters and learn a bit about the Chinese calendar and what animal represents the current year and the year in which each of us was born. These are fascinating concepts for the kindergartners. The children can make red gift envelopes using shiny red paper. After the children trace and cut out a patterned shape, we sit with small groups and show them how to fold the shiny triangles into envelopes. We tape the envelopes on three sides and then have the children slip in small chocolate coins, which symbolize the money that is traditionally given. We then seal the envelopes and the children bring them home to share and teach their families about the Chinese New Year.

We know schools that have a parade for Chinese New Year. The sixth graders do all the preparations for the parade and then as they walk through the school, the younger students line the hallways to watch the parade. Many classes make things to create a festive atmosphere throughout the school. One first-grade class made a huge dragon from paper, paint, and glitter to hang outside their classroom.

We have had parades in our own classrooms. Another symbol of the new year is a lantern or a scary mask. Both are thought to scare away the evil monsters. After the class makes masks or lanterns the children each choose a noisy instrument, line up, and parade around the room to festive music. It is always exciting to learn about customs and traditions that are different from our own.

New Routines

January is a good time to start some more advanced routines in our morning meeting. Bonnie begins to count one hundred days of school in January. Her school year ends late in June so there is still enough time to count one hundred days of school. She begins by putting a Popsicle stick in a box for each day and bundling them in rubber bands when they reach ten, twenty, thirty, and so on. By using a counting board, Bonnie clearly represents the concept of ones, tens, and eventually hundreds so children can better understand place value.

We also begin a number line for counting to one hundred. We like to do it in strips of ten. This helps the children see a pattern as we count to one hundred. There are entire books devoted to one hundred days of school and related routines and concepts. We choose a few valuable routines and follow through. We know this concept will be taught again in subsequent elementary grades and we are laying the foundation.

January is also a good time to begin observing and recording the weather. We like to start a large graph. In a half-day kindergarten, the morning class records the weather with a blue sticker and the afternoon records it with a red one, and

Figure 6–3. Bonnie counts the days of school on a counting board.

after a few weeks the children can begin to draw some conclusions about the weather. We continue the graph until the end of the year, so we use a large piece of paper or posterboard for this project.

Science Museum

During the winter, Bonnie sets up a science museum in the classroom. This is very popular and not that hard to do. It can be simple or quite elaborate. Areas in the science museum can be set up so the children can experiment in different ways. She usually has about four different concepts represented at a time and then rotates new ones in as the children tire of older ones. Some of the exhibits that have been successful are space exploration, magnets, toys that spin, colors, dinosaurs, oceans, bones, shadows, sounds, bubbles, and nature. The nature exhibit includes things Bonnie has collected, such as snake skins, a turtle shell, wasps' nests, volcanic rocks, a turkey wing, a cow skull, and a cow spine. For each

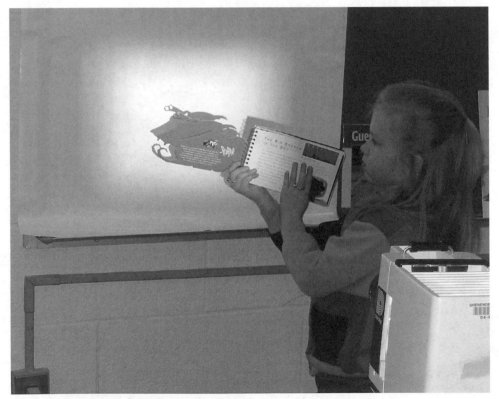

Figure 6–4. Making shadows in the science museum

of these exhibits, she collects toys, posters, puzzles, and books that relate to the topic. The key is to make it as interactive as possible. For instance, for shadows, she sets up an old filmstrip projector so the children can make shadows on a wall. She also asks parents to send in objects to share that are related to these topics.

Summary

When the children come back to school after the holiday break, many look taller and more filled out. They are more capable with tying, zipping, and putting on their boots, gloves, and mittens. The children are visibly more mature than when they began kindergarten. Developmentally, it is an important juncture and a good time to update the assessments. In our experience, most children have now acquired many concepts and skills that they didn't know in the fall. It is reassuring to look at a fall handwriting sample of a child's name and compare it with a current one. Much growth and progress have occurred. The children can play more independently and plan their own games and activities at choice time. They are taking turns, sharing toys, responding with empathy, and generally are better able to solve a problem or work out a temporary solution. That's not to say we don't have some tattling and whining about who will be first (and sometimes even last) in line or difficulty with sharing, but most children seem more able to cope with these trials and tribulations.

There is only one school holiday in January, for Martin Luther King Day, so if we are not interrupted by snow days, we have more time with the children. This is terrific since each school day is an opportunity to strengthen the emerging competencies of each child in the class.

February

Delving Deeper

By February, we are all feeling like old friends. We know the children well and they have gotten to know us. Their sense of humor is developing and we have some good laughs. The routines and procedures that we have developed are humming right along now. The children show independence and they have taken ownership of the classroom. For the most part the children know how to work and play with each other and they can negotiate, share, and take turns.

Therefore, the children who are still struggling socially and academically are putting up red flags for some extra support. We have tried several approaches by now and it may be time for a closer look from our school's child study team. This team includes the school psychologist, speech teacher, counselor, principal, special education teachers, a classroom teacher, and the teacher who is seeking advice.

We do a theme on friendship this month and set up a class post office and celebrate Valentine's Day. We have a week's vacation during February, so the month flies right by. When we return from the break at the end of the month, we expect the children will do more writing and many have become emergent readers. They are more articulate and able to speak up in a group. It's very satisfying to see these changes.

At-Risk Students

Because kindergartners are often the youngest children in our schools and have no prior school history, it takes a while to get to know them. Some schools have pre-K programs, so the children may have been in school the previous year. Even so, it is difficult to identify the reasons a child is not developing on schedule at such an early age. It takes some time to determine whether the lag or delay a student is showing is developmental, due to a lack of prior exposure to certain concepts and skills, or a school adjustment issue. There are a number of ways to support the student who is at risk.

In our schools there are some effective supports to assist children with learning disabilities or developmental delays. At Debra's school the Connections Program is designed for a small group of children who have been identified as needing support services. The Connections Program delivers services such as speech therapy, occupational therapy, physical therapy, and social work through seasonal or theme-related activities and events.

There is a similar program called Extended Day Kindergarten for designated children at Bonnie's school. The Extended Day Kindergarten portion of the day is limited to twelve students selected from four kindergarten classes.

We are fortunate to also have reading staff in our schools to support children who are having difficulty with letter identification, letter sounds, and basic sight words and all children who are generally delayed in literacy development. Support staff work with small groups in sessions lasting about fifteen minutes three times a week. Additional small-group instruction targeting certain skills can be very effective in kindergarten. We believe early intervention is critical, and currently there are more mandates and program initiatives for kindergarten than ever before.

Phonemic Awareness

We both began our careers in the mid-'70s and have been in education long enough to observe some patterns and changes. Shall we say we have seen the pendulum swing back and forth a few times. It is these years of teaching early literacy combined with keeping up-to-date on research and current thinking about literacy that drive our comments and practices regarding phonemic awareness.

Phonemic awareness is an understanding that language is composed of small units of speech called phonemes that correspond to the letters of an alphabetic writing system. For instance, /b/ is the phoneme that represents the letter *b* in the word *butterfly*. And phonics is the system by which symbols represent sounds in an alphabetic writing system.

"Children who are phonemically aware can think about and manipulate sounds in words. They know when words rhyme or do not; they know when words begin or end with the same sound; and they know a word like *bat* is composed of three sounds /b/ /a/ /t/ and that these sounds can be blended into a spoken word" (Neuman, Copple, and Bredekamp 2000).

In *Phonemic Awareness in Young Children* (Adams et al. 1998), the authors have a systematic approach to teaching phonemic awareness. We recommend reading this book for a more complete explanation of phonemic awareness. Many teachers already integrate much of what the authors recommend in the context of everyday routines. Reading stories to the children, rhyming, and writing and reading the daily message together are perfect for teaching phonemic awareness. Teachers who are not yet experienced or knowledgeable about early literacy may benefit from using the exercises and games in *Phonemic Awareness in Young Children*.

We think it is important to keep phonemic awareness instruction in perspective because it is only one of many cueing strategies children use while reading and because about 75 percent of students will acquire phonemic awareness without direct instruction. Therefore, we recommend teaching phonemic awareness in the context of meaningful routines and by using brief whole-class minilessons for approximately the first half of the school year. The children who are struggling with these skills in late winter can receive small-group direct instruction in phonemeic awareness from the classroom teacher or support staff.

Reading aloud to children is still the single most important activity for building understandings and skills essential for reading success (Wells 1985). We also recommend *Learning to Read and Write: Developmentally Appropriate Practices for Young Children*, by Neuman, Copple, and Bredekamp (2000). This book is full of developmentally appropriate ways to teach literacy and explains the research that drives these practices.

Following is a bibliography of rhyming books and predictable books that help children develop phonemic awareness. Simple techniques such as having the children fill in rhyming words as you read, playing with language, and substituting initial consonants all build phonemic awareness in a playful and natural way.

Rhyming Books

Alarcon, K. B. 1997. *Louella Mae, She's Run Away!* New York: Henry Holt.

Alborough, J. 1992. *Where's My Teddy?* Cambridge, MA: Candlewick.

Brown, M. 1985. *Hand Rhymes*. London: Picture Lions.

———. 1987. *Play Rhymes*. New York: E. P. Dutton.

Carter, D. A. 1992. *Over in the Meadow*. New York: Scholastic.

Cowley, J. 1987. *Dan, the Flying Man*. San Diego: Wright Group.

———. 1996. *Nicketty-Nacketty Noo-Noo-Noo*. Greenvale, NY: Mondo.

Dodd, L. 1983. *Hairy Maclary from Donaldson's Dairy*. New York: Trumpet Club.

Ehlert, L. 1990. *Feathers for Lunch*. New York: Trumpet Club.

———. 2001. *Waiting for Wings*. New York: Harcourt.

Fox, M. 1996. *Boo to a Goose*. New York: Puffin.

Gelman, R. 1992. *More Spaghetti, I Say!* New York: Scholastic.

Maccarone, G. 1994. *Oink! Moo! How Do You Do?* New York: Scholastic.

Martin, B. J. 1989. *Chicka Chicka Boom Boom.* New York: Scholastic.

Prater, J. 1993. *Once Upon a Time.* Cambridge, MA: Candlewick.

Riley, L. 1997. *Mouse Mess.* New York: Scholastic.

Weeks, S. 1998. *Mrs. McNosh Hangs Up Her Wash.* New York: Harper Festival.

Wood, A. 1982. *Quick as a Cricket.* New York: Scholastic.

Yolen, J. 2003. *How Do Dinosaurs Get Well Soon?* New York: Blue Sky.

Predictable and Pattern Books

Cowley, J. 1980. *Mrs. Wishy-Washy Big book.* San Diego: Wright Group.

———. 1987. *The Jigaree.* San Diego: Wright Group.

———. 1987. *The Farm Concert.* San Diego: Wright Group.

———. 1987. *Hairy Bear.* San Diego: Wright Group.

———. 1987. *To Town.* San Diego: Wright Group.

———. 1988. *Smarty Parts.* San Diego: Wright Group.

———. 1996. *Nicketty-Nacketty Noo-Noo-Noo.* Greenvale, NY: Mondo.

Fox, M. 1996. *Zoo-Looking.* New York: Scholastic.

Hutchins, P. 1972. *Good-Night Owl!* New York: Trumpet Club.

Kalan, R. 1981. *Jump, Frog, Jump!* New York: Scholastic.

Martin, B. J. 1992. *Brown Bear, Brown Bear, What Do You See?* New York: Holt, Rhinehart and Winston.

McGovern, A. 1967. *Too Much Noise.* Boston: Houghton Mifflin.

Wood, A. 1994. *Quick as a Cricket.* New York: Scholastic.

February Themes

Friendship

The month of February lends itself naturally to focusing on friends and friendship. When thinking about a theme on friendship, we first pull together all the literature. A good book to begin with is *How to Be a Friend,* by Laurie Krasny Brown and Marc Brown (1998). It is comprehensive and playful. We read it in two or three sittings because we need time to discuss and role-play the information. It lends itself to many extension activities such as writing, drawing, and puppets. *How to Lose All Your Friends,* by Nancy Carlson (1994), is another book we use for this theme. It is a springboard to interesting discussions and follow-up activities.

Some of the songs we learn during this theme are "We All Sing with the Same Voice" (2001), by Miller and Greene, which comes packaged as a book and a CD. This is one of the favorites for the entire year. There is also a great song and dance called "Jump Jim Joe" on a CD by the same name (New England Dancing Masters 1991) that can be obtained through the Amidons' website at *www.amidonmusic.com.*

The children paint and draw pictures of their friends and work on handwriting while writing classmates' names. They learn new board and card games to play and do math activities with friends.

Books on Friendship

Bourgeois, P. 1997. *Franklin's New Friend*. New York: Scholastic.

Brown, L. K., and M. Brown. 1998. *How to Be a Friend*. Boston: Little, Brown.

Bunnett, R. 1995. *Friends at School*. New York: Scholastic.

Carlson, N. 1988. *I Like Me!* New York: Trumpet Club.

———. 1994. *How to Lose All Your Friends*. New York: Viking.

Clements, A. 1988. *Big Al*. New York: Scholastic.

Henkes, K. 1989. *Jessica*. New York: Puffin.

———. 1991. *Chrysanthemum*. New York: William Morrow.

Mayer, M. 1987. *There's an Alligator Under My Bed*. New York: Dial Books for Young Readers.

———. 1988. *Just My Friend and Me*. New York: Golden.

McBratney, S. 2001. *I'll Always Be Your Friend*. New York: Harper Collins.

Figure 7–1. Friends with drawings of friends

Figure 7–2. Writing friends' names

Miller, P., and Greene, S. (2001). *We All Sing with the Same Voice*. New York: Harper Collins.

Raschka, C. 1993. *Yo! Yes!* New York: Scholastic.

———. 2000. *Ring! Yo?* New York: Dorling Kindersley.

Roddie, S. 1998. *Too Close Friends*. New York: Dial Books for Young Readers.

Sathre, V. 1997. *Three Kind Mice*. New York: Harcourt Brace.

Saxton, F., and J. Elffers. 1999. *How Are You Peeling? Foods with Moods*. New York: Arthur A. Levine.

Tafuri, N. 2000. *Shy Charles*. New York: Scholastic.

Wells, R. 1995a. *Edward in Deep Water*. New York: Dial Books for Young Readers.

———. 1995b. *Edward's Overwhelming Overnight*. New York: Dial Books for Young Readers.

Post Office and Valentine's Day

We set up a post office in the classroom in preparation for Valentine's Day. The post office inspires the children to write notes and letters to each other. And when Valentine's Day rolls around, they love to "mail" their Valentines. Learning about the post office is a logical extension of a theme on friendship and Valentine's Day.

Figure 7–3. Delivering Valentines in the post office

If you are unable to take a field trip to a post office, Fisher-Price produces a series of videos called Terrific Trips that are each about fifteen minutes long. One of them is about a trip to a post office and is very informative; it follows the journey of a letter mailed by a little boy to his grandma. The children see the entire process from door to door.

After writing short letters to his friends and mailing them in our classroom post office, each child makes a large picture postcard to mail to his family. The children illustrate one side of a $5\frac{1}{2}$-by-$8\frac{1}{2}$-inch piece of oak tag and write the address and message on the other side. It's very exciting for the children to see their post-cards arrive with the mail at home.

The songs "Mail Myself to You," by Woodie Guthrie, and "Skidamarink" are both on the *Teaching Kindergarten* CDs (Walmsley, Camp, and Walmsley 1992b) and go well with the Valentine's Day and post office theme. "Mail Myself to You" has three verses, so we generally teach just the chorus, but as we sing it

Figure 7–4. Front and back of postcard

again and again, the children begin to learn the verses as well. We always have the songs on charts with picture clues. The children do the illustrations with our guidance. And we add motions to most songs to keep the children actively involved.

A couple of stories we enjoy reading for Valentine's Day are *Roses Are Pink, Your Feet Really Stink*, by Diane deGroat (1996), and *Valentine Bears*, by Eve Bunting (1983). *I Love You, Good Night*, by Jon Buller and Susan Schade (1998), is a good springboard to making a patterned class book about things the children love. Another good book is *Emily's Valentine Party*, by Claire Masurel (1999). This is a lift-the-flap book and they are always popular in the class library.

Books About Valentine's Day and Post Offices

Brown, M. 1980. *Arthur's Valentine*. Boston: Little, Brown.
Buller, J., and S. Schrade. 1988. *I Love You, Good Night*. New York: Little Simon.
Bunting, E. 1983. *Valentine Bears*. New York: Clarion.
Carter, D. 2003. *Love Bugs*. New York: Little Simon.
deGroat, D. 1996. *Roses Are Pink, Your Feet Really Stink*. New York: Mulberry.
Guthrie, W. 1994. *Mail Myself to You: Let Me Read*. Glenview, IL: Scott Foresman.
Masurel, C. 1999. *Emily's Valentine Party*. New York: Puffin.

Money

We have found February to be a good time to begin learning about money. Our goal is for the children to identify the penny, nickel, dime, and quarter and to learn their values. We like to integrate this with learning about Washington and Lincoln. We celebrate Presidents' Day in February, so what better time to talk about George and Abe and find them on the penny and the quarter?

We read a few books about Washington and Lincoln and have pictures of them in the classroom. We do get a day off from school to celebrate Presidents' Day, so we like the children to know about these presidents.

It is fun to put out different coins and magnifying glasses for the children to get a closer look. Putting the coins on a large piece of black felt makes them show up nicely and keeps the activity rather quiet and prevents the coins from rolling off the table. The children are very interested in the dates, words, and pictures on the coins. The activity can be extended by asking the children to find specific numbers, words, and pictures on the coins, for example, the number six, George Washington, or a word they know. One way we help children distinguish between various sizes and thicknesses of coins is to have them place each coin in their hands and then put their hands behind their backs. As we hold up a coin the children try to match it by feeling the coins behind their backs. They love to see if they can identify the correct coin by touch. Try it yourself!

Summary

Here in the Northeast we have a week's vacation from school in mid-February. This originally began during the first oil embargo so schools could save on heating costs, and it has remained ever since. Now it coincides with Presidents' Day. It is nice to have that week off from school, because unlike the December break, there are no holiday pressures.

February break is a good time to reorganize some parts of the classroom, look at new materials, and do all the things it is impossible to tackle when preparing for the children every day. If we do not have travel plans that take us away to visit friends or family, then we can often be found sitting quietly and thoughtfully in our classrooms, contemplating changes that would be beneficial for the second half of the school year. Putting on good music, organizing materials and books, cleaning out areas that have become cluttered, or planning a new theme or project is very rewarding. There are few times when we have the luxury of quiet contemplation in our classrooms. We may even take a trip to the local bookstore to peruse the new books and place an order. If the opportunity arises, a trip to a tropical island or to the mountains to ski can also rejuvenate a weary kindergarten teacher.

After a welcome break, it is a good time to make a plan regarding children we believe are struggling academically and socially. In our schools we have to fill out some paperwork before any child can be considered by the child study team. This is a good time to do that as well. As the end of February arrives, the days are noticeably longer and we are hopeful that spring may be around the corner.

March

Capable, Confident, and Constructive

In our experience, March is a developmental milestone in kindergarten for most children. These are not the "babies" that we met in September. Many have turned six and they are starting to look more like first graders every day. In March we're thinking ahead to the end of the school year and even planning for the following year. We begin thinking about end-of-the-year celebrations, and this is the month we have registration and meet the next year's incoming children and parents.

Looking Ahead

Registration and Orientation

Many private and public schools designate March as the month to register kindergartners for the following school year. We may be asked to make a presentation to our incoming parents about our kindergarten program and invite these children and their families to school in the spring prior to beginning kindergarten.

There are many ways to do this. We want to address the parents and welcome the children. This can be done with two separate programs or by inviting parents and children at the same time and providing a program for parents while the children visit the classrooms.

We have several objectives when meeting with parents. First, we work with the principal to welcome the parents to the school and share the district's philosophy on kindergarten. There are also the logistics of bus schedules, cafeteria, health physicals, and so on that need to be addressed. Perhaps the nurse, speech teacher, and counselor will want to say a few words.

Kindergarten teachers can address the parents on topics such as

- what parents can do in the upcoming months to help their children be more comfortable with and confident about starting school
- suggestions for family fun and learning
- tips on television and reading together
- where to seek advice if parents have concerns about their children's development

A PowerPoint slide show or a video of a day in kindergarten can be narrated by one of the kindergarten teachers. As parents leave the large gathering space, they can casually tour the kindergarten classrooms.

In Debra's district, two days are designated for the children to walk through the classrooms and for parents to officially register their children. On these days class is in session. Therefore, these visiting days are a bit hectic, but since she knows that in advance, Debra is well prepared. Parents are welcome to informally walk into the classroom and see what is going on and get a flavor for how the program is set up and what it will be like for their children as kindergartners. Most parents stay about fifteen minutes. It is helpful to take some notes on those children or families that may present a need in some way or have asked Debra a question related to services or readiness.

In Bonnie's school, the incoming kindergartners come to visit the classrooms and teachers after school is dismissed. The children play with some toys, meet the teachers, have a look around, and take a bus ride. (All children in her district ride the school bus.) She tries to note anything that may require some follow-up, such as a child needing a speech evaluation, social services, or just some reassurance. The counselor, psychologist, speech teacher, and nurse are there to assist.

Some schools do a formal screening in the spring before children enter kindergarten. Our school districts do not. See the August chapter for more about screenings.

Closing Celebration

In Debra's district, each kindergarten class plans a program for the end of the year. This is a good time for us to choose the songs, dances, stories, and poems to be used so we do not have to scramble to teach new ones for the closing performance. This way the performance is truly a celebration of what the children have learned throughout the year.

An end-of-the-year celebration is a wonderful way to remember all of the happy and special times we have had together as a class. Parents, grandparents, and other close family relatives or friends love to come to school and see their children participate. If this program is a celebration of the kinds of things done all year in class, then it is a relatively stress-free event. Children perform songs, poems, stories, and dances they have chosen. March is the time to introduce any new songs or dances that we think might become favorites so the children have enough time to learn them and feel comfortable with them before the closing performance. That way if we add signing or some simple props to a dance, song, or story, it is a small adjustment and not a major undertaking.

The children can create beautiful scenery in the style of Eric Carle and Lois Ehlert by making "pretty paper" (described in May in the "Painting" section). Because the children create the scenery, program, and small props and choose the pieces to perform, it becomes their celebration. It is a joyful day when all the parents and other family members come together to share excitement, laughter, tears, and love. This is a big day for the children and their families. After the performance everyone is invited back to the classroom, outside, or the gym to have refreshments. A parent or two can organize the refreshments and leave the teacher free to visit with families. Warm and fond feelings abound on this day!

Figure 8–1. Closing celebration scenery

Bedtime and Bathtime Theme

March is a long month uninterrupted by holidays. There is time to get immersed in a theme or project. One of Bonnie's favorite themes in March is bedtime and bathtime. It has an abundance of good literature and certain health-related topics are easily integrated: getting plenty of rest, proper hygiene, and dental health. It is also a good way to introduce the concept of telling time and learning about clocks. There are also many counting books that fit nicely with this theme.

The children enjoy bringing bathtub toys to share and these can be set up by the sink or at a water table. We provide smocks so we don't end up sending wet children home on a chilly day in March. Kindergartners also like to bring some of the stuffed animals and dolls that they sleep with to school. These items create many opportunities for speaking, writing, listening, counting, and sorting.

A good starting point for this theme is to read the big book *Sing a Song* (1980), published by the Wright Group. The accompanying audiotape provides the music and is a delightful addition to the book. Some other books that are winners for this theme are *The Napping House* and *King Bidgood's in the Bathtub*, by Audrey Wood (1984, 1993). Occasionally Bonnie asks parents if anyone would like to make a flannel board kit that relates to a particular story, and she has two sets for *The Napping House* that the children use to retell the story. *Ira Sleeps Over, Arthur's First Sleepover, D. W.'s Lost Blankie, Time for Bed, Bedtime for Frances,* and *Lazy Mary* (1980) (big book by the Wright Group) are also must-reads for this theme.

Bedtime and Bathtime Books

Brown, M. 1997. *Goodnight Moon*. New York: HarperCollins.
Brown, M. 1994. *Arthur's First Sleepover*. Boston: Little, Brown.
———. 1998. *D. W.'s Lost Blankie*. Boston: Little, Brown.
Christelow, E. 1989. *Five Little Monkeys Jumping on the Bed*. New York: Trumpet Club.
Dunbar, J. 1998. *Tell Me Something Happy Before I Go to Sleep*. New York: Scholastic.
Hoban, R. 1996. *Bedtime for Frances*. New York: Harper Collins.
Fox, M. 1993. *Time for Bed*. New York: Trumpet Club.
Melsert, J. 1987. *Lazy Mary*. San Diego: Wright Group.
———. 1987. *Sing a Song*. San Diego: Wright Group.
Rees, M. 1988. *Ten in a Bed*. Boston: Little, Brown.
Spinelli, E. 2000. *When Mama Comes Home Tonight*. New York: Scholastic.
Waber, B. 1972. *Ira Sleeps Over*. Boston: Houghton Mifflin.
Walton, R. 1998. *So Many Bunnies: A Bedtime ABC and Counting Book*. New York: Scholastic.
Wood, A. 1984. *The Napping House*. New York: Harcourt Brace Jovanovich.

———. 1993. *King Bidgood's in the Bathtub.* New York: Scholastic.
Yolen, J. 2001. *How Do Dinosaurs Say Good Night?* New York: Scholastic.
Zolotow, C. 1988. *Sleepy Book.* New York: Harper and Row.

Some songs that go well with this theme are "Brush Your Teeth," by Raffi, "Sing a Song," which goes with Wright Group big book, and "Dreams of Harmony," which can be found on one of the CDs that go with *Teaching Kindergarten.* In the latter song, Mary Alice Amidon sings "good night" in many different languages.

Math lends itself to being integrated into this theme, and we have included some of the books we have used to teach math in this theme in the list on page 125. While reading *Ten in a Bed* (Rees 1988) and *Five Little Monkeys* (Christelow 1989), we count backward, which is a natural introduction to subtraction.

Time

We want children to begin to associate things we do with the different times of day when we do them so they understand time as a concept rather than just numbers on a clock. We make number cards for one through twelve and put them in a circle on the floor like a huge clock, then we have two children (one taller and

Figure 8–2. Kids are the clock

one shorter) be the hands on the clock and move around to indicate different times. We focus on time to the hour.

Two books we use to teach telling time are *Little Rabbit's First Time Book*, by Alan Baker (1999) and *Time To . . .*, by Bruce McMillan (1989). As you read either of these books, each child can follow with her own movable teaching clock, moving the hands to match each page in the book as you read it.

Books on Time

Baker, A. 1999. *Little Rabbit's First Time Book*. New York: Kingfisher.
Hutchins, P. 1995. *Clocks and More Clocks*. New York: Scholastic.
McMillan, B. 1989. *Time To . . . .* New York: Scholastic.

We also graph our bedtimes. We found it interesting that Bonnie actually goes to bed before some of the children! We send home a paper to help children learn the difference between analog and digital clocks and watches. As an informal homework, we ask the children to count all the digital and analog clocks and watches in their homes. A good story to read about clocks is *Clocks and More Clocks*, by Pat Hutchins (1995).

An interesting activity is to ask each child to paint a picture of herself in her bed or in the bathtub and later have her dictate a story about her picture as an adult types it into the computer. Then we can print them and attach their stories to their paintings and compile them into a collaborative class book.

Dental Health

As we begin learning about dental health, *How Many Teeth?* (Showers 1991) is a great book to start with. It gives age-appropriate information and weaves a story and some poems throughout. If you haven't already done it, this is a good time to start a lost teeth graph or chart. We invite a dentist or hygienist to talk to the children and have often been able to get each child a free toothbrush and toothpaste as well. We have made a worksheet on which each child can count and record the number of teeth he currently has, how many he has lost, and how many are currently loose.

Books About Teeth

Brown, M. 1985. *Arthur's Tooth*. New York: Little, Brown.
Middleton, C. 2001. *Tabitha's Terrifically Tough Tooth*. New York:
    Phyllis Fogelman.
Showers, P. 1991. *How Many Teeth?* New York: Scholastic.

The children enjoy ending this theme with a pajama party. We all wear pj's to school and bring a favorite stuffed animal. We also ask each child to bring a small shoe box to use the day of the pajama party to make a toy bed. We put two

This is a picture of me taking a shower.
Sometimes I take a bath. Then I get out.
Danny

Figure 8–3. Danny's page from "Bedtime and Bathtime" book

clothespins (not the spring kind) on a shoe box to serve as posts at the head of the bed. If money is no object, go wild and make four-poster beds! We have the children decorate the beds with markers and paint. The children like to glue beads on top of the clothespins and draw and put stickers on the shoe boxes. It is very open-ended. We have some precut fabric for sheets and blankets and pillows. Then the children can just add their favorite beanbag animal, doll, or small stuffed animal.

We also watch a short video on the day of the pajama party and make it a special movie event by serving popcorn. Often the children will draw and write about the pajamas or slippers they are wearing or the stuffed animals they like to sleep with. We sort and graph the pj's or slippers we are wearing as well as the types of stuffed animals the children brought to school.

Summary

March is a long school month without any designated holidays and a very busy month because of spring registration, orientation for new families, and the second set of parent-teacher conferences. Debra's school district allows for two planned

Figure 8–4. Bonnie reads to the children during the class pajama party.

opportunities to meet with parents and the second set of conferences is held in March. March is also a wonderful time to do an in-depth theme or project.

Because the children have matured and demonstrated much cognitive growth since the start of school, this is a good time to address some more advanced math concepts, such as time and basic subtraction. It is also an appropriate time to expect more from the children in academic, social, and emotional domains. In March we begin to look at each child with an eye toward her adjustment to and success in first grade.

If we are still seeing children with big gaps in the kindergarten assessment, it is time to take another look at the type and amount of support we are giving them. We request a meeting with our child study team to plan a course of action. We inform parents about our concerns and efforts to help their children. Sometimes a parent will not or cannot work with us to help her child. If that is the case, then we make the decision to do all we can in the school setting, using as many resources as possible.

April

Feeling Like a Family

By April the children are very different than when we first met them in September. Most are now confident, lively, and independent. We continue to raise our expectations for their work and skill development. Themes on fairy tales and folktales, famous artists, farm animals, and the egg-to-chick cycle are all great topics we have explored in spring.

Writing Revisited Again

By this time of year, the children have had a great deal of writing experience, so we start to

- offer more varieties of writing paper
- offer numerous styles and sizes of blank books
- see more ending sounds as well as initial sounds for words
- see a few words spelled correctly and some very close approximations

Words like *and, the, end, is, it, mom, dad, love, I, no,* and *yes* appear in the children's writing. The children begin to spell these words correctly because we have repeatedly used them in our classroom when doing the morning message, reading books, working on themes and projects, and writing and reading song charts. Many of these words are on the high-frequency word list that our district would like kindergartners and early first graders to master.

We are now working with children on using spaces between their words. In our classes, we give each student a simple wooden clothespin with a sticker of an astronaut, or spaceman on it that we purchased from the Really Good Stuff catalog.

After writing each word, the child places a "spaceman" and begins the next word on the other side of the clothespin. Additionally, we

- show how capital letters begin many writing lines
- talk about and use the period more
- show the question mark and the exclamation point
- show speech clouds
- show and use more sophisticated labels on drawings
- model and see longer writing pieces
- model and see more short books with a definite beginning, middle, and ending
- look for more concept books, such as alphabet books (with a theme of food, toys, animals, etc.), weekend adventures, holiday happenings, pet stories, number books, joke books, how-to books, sequence books, compare-and-contrast structures, and other nonfiction writing

Through daily writing integrated throughout the subject areas and writers workshop, we have seen much growth in the children's writing since the start of the school year.

Toward the end of the school year, we hold an authors celebration, for which each child completes a special piece to be shared or we write a class book in which each child creates a separate page and then we share it. We have a reception with book buddies, parents, or other guests where we share and enjoy writing pieces from the year.

In Debra's class the children work with their third-grade book buddies during a young author celebration. The event starts off with Debra reading a Caldecott book. Then the class has a short discussion about what makes a Caldecott book so good. Each kindergartner along with her book buddy reads through her writing folder and together they look at the writing pieces and notice the growth and changes since September. The third graders guide their kindergarten buddies in looking for the piece that is an award winner in each child's folder. Some of the criteria would be

- created great detailed illustrations
- told a long story or made a longer book
- used lots of color
- used lots of words
- wrote about just one topic
- created some of the best work done by that child

You can order or make inexpensive ribbons to award the kindergartners' best books. Debra's class ends this authors reception by reading a collaborative class book and then enjoying some refreshments.

Figure 9–1. Spring writing samples show many more whole words, lively and colorful illustrations, and longer stories: "I was excited because today is my birthday. / I had Kelly and Jen over for my birthday. / Now my birthday was over. / It was a good time. / Now it is nighttime. I go to bed."

More Money

In April, Bonnie revisits the topic of money and sets up a variety store in the classroom to help the children learn the names and values of the coins. Early in the year she asks parents to collect any little trinkets, cheap jewelry, toys, freebies, or giveaways from fast-food restaurants that kindergartners might like. She begins by pricing items at two cents and three cents and giving the children each five pennies to shop with. Each time they shop, Bonnie puts out items that are priced a little higher and gives each child more money until they get to the twenty-five-cent items. Bonnie saves these items for the final shopping day. There is always plenty of merchandise because parents of students from previous years save what the students bought at WalmsleyMart and return it to Bonnie to sell again. Talk about recycling!

Let's Find Out About Money, by Kathy Barabas, is a great book that shows children how coins are made. *Jelly Beans for Sale,* by Bruce McMillan (1996), is another great book for kindergartners. It has vibrant color photos. *Benny's Pennies,* by Pat Brisson (1993), is a third book we recommend for teaching about money.

Money Books

Barabas, K. 1997. *Let's Find Out About Money.* New York: Scholastic.
Brisson, P. 1993. *Benny's Pennies.* New York: Bantam Doubleday Dell.
McMillan, B. 1996. *Jelly Beans for Sale.* New York: Scholastic.

Egg-to-Chick Theme

The egg-to-chick cycle is a wonderful theme to do in the spring. Where we live, we can obtain fertilized eggs from the local chapter of the Cornell Cooperative Extension. If you don't have a similar organization that supports farmers and gardeners in your area, just find a farmer who has some chickens and a rooster! Many science catalogs also provide fertilized eggs and incubators. For teachers who plan to hatch chicks each year, an incubator might be a worthwhile investment. Follow the directions that come with the incubator carefully. The eggs need to be turned daily and the temperature needs to remain between 99 and 101 degrees. After the eggs are in the incubator for five or six days, we hold the eggs in front of the light of an old filmstrip projector to see how many eggs are developing. If an egg is fertilized and developing, two dark spots where the heart and eyes are and small red blood vessels will be visible. It is a thrill to see the chick developing inside the egg.

One year Bonnie had a power failure at her school over a weekend and at the end of the twenty-one days, no chicks hatched. She realized they were not going to hatch and knew a teacher in the district with a couple of newly hatched chicks to spare, and miraculously they appeared in the incubator in Bonnie's classroom, complete with cracked eggshells. Routinely, two or three out of a dozen don't hatch and it is not a problem. But when none of the eggs hatch, it calls for drastic measures!

After the chicks hatch, we keep them for only a few days before sending them off to a farm since they are very noisy, a bit smelly, and begin to fly out of the box. We have hatched chicks year after year and it is truly a highlight for the children and us. We care for the eggs for twenty-one days by turning them and keeping them moist and warm, and we count down the days, candle the eggs, and read, write, and sketch about them. We are all ecstatic when the chicks finally start pecking their way out of their shells. This is an experience children remember for years to come.

Egg-to-Chick Books

Back, C. 1984. *Chicken and Egg*. New York: Trumpet Club.

Boylston, A. 1998. *Life Cycle of a Chicken*. Chicago: Heinemann. (Also available as a big book.)

Burton, R. 1994. *Egg: A Photographic Story of Hatching*. New York: Dorling Kindersley.

Heller, R. 1981. *Chickens Aren't the Only Ones*. New York: Scholastic.

Jeunesse, G. 1989. *The Egg*. New York: Scholastic.

McMillan, B. 1983. *Here a Chick, There a Chick*. New York: Trumpet Club.

Min, L. 1994. *Mrs. Sato's Hens*. Glenview, IL: Scott Foresman.

Selsam, M. E. 1970. *Egg to Chick*. New York: Harper Collins.

Wells, R. 1989. *Max's Chocolate Chicken*. New York: Scholastic.

Williams, G. 1992. *The Chicken Book*. New York: Dell.

Figure 9–2. Children turning the eggs.

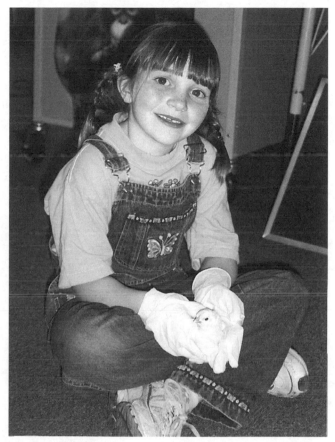

Figure 9–3. The chicks hatched!

Summary

What a lovely month April is. We have become a strong community of learners and feel like a family. We know each other quite well. By now most children can work around differences and find solutions to their problems. The classroom feels like a second home for all of us. We have spent many hours together, sharing, discovering, and learning through books, hands-on experiences, trips, and visiting speakers. But most of all we have learned so much from each other this year in kindergarten.

When we began writing in September, it was challenging and at times tedious work. Now most of the children embrace writing time as a way to be creative and enjoy personal expression. They also love to share their writing pieces and there are many more volunteers who want to share their stories than slots available each day.

If we are successful with our egg incubation, the children and we are euphoric on the day they begin to peck out of their shells. Although the life cycle of twenty-one days is not a very long time, it feels like we have watched over our eggs forever. When the chicks start to hatch, we suspend our regular activities to allow the children to post signs up and down our hallway. We stop to tell the great news to first- or second-grade friends and then make a group announcement over the P.A. system as part of the morning news. This happy and special event strengthens the strong bonds we have been forming all year long.

May

Well on Their Way

May is a terrific time to get back outside again and do more outdoor activities. Teachers living in warmer climates can't imagine how exciting this can be. When talking to colleagues in California and Hawaii, it boggles our minds to think of eating lunch, working, and playing outdoors year-round! For us, the leaves are just returning to the trees, piles of snow have recently melted, and the grass is turning green once again. Finally, we can leave our homes without boots, gloves, scarves, hats, and winter coats. We can just head out the door to the playground.

Gardening

If we have started seeds indoors as part of a science or spring activity, now we can plant them with the children in a garden. The children love to plant, water, and tend their bit of the garden. Debra expands her garden varieties even more by asking parents and colleagues to send in any bulbs or divided perennials they don't need. Some annual flowers for instant color are a big hit with the children. A collection of small hand shovels works well for the children to use for planting. If we demonstrate digging in the garden and gently putting plants in the holes and watering them, the children can successfully follow our model.

We have a friend and colleague, Abby Weber, who has an extensive garden outside her kindergarten classroom. One spring, Abby's kindergarten class did a project on gardens. She selected gardens as the topic for several reasons. The country setting of her school provides wonderful opportunities for nature studies of all types. Right outside the kindergarten classroom is a courtyard that can be seen from the classroom. The classroom also has a door that goes directly to the garden. The kindergarten science curriculum includes a unit on the life cycle of plants. Abby thought that doing a project that involved planning, preparing, planting, and caring for a real garden would give the children a much richer and more authentic experience with plants and their life cycles than planting seeds in paper cups and watching them grow in the classroom.

As the weather turned warmer the children became very excited about the changes they were observing outside both at home and at school. The children began coming to school with fists full of dandelions and other flowers picked from yards and gardens at home. The children discovered crocuses, tulips, and daffodils sprouting in the courtyard outside the classroom. They began observing and representing the flowers with great excitement as they grew from sprouts to full blooms. It became clear that plants was a topic of great interest to the children.

Abby shared the idea of doing a garden project with the children during a group meeting. Abby had taken digital photographs of the courtyard area from the time children had discovered the sprouting bulbs. Using these photographs, along with some of the children's observational sketches, they began discussing their experiences with plants both at school and at home. With the help of a wonderful school custodian, Abby took photographs of the courtyard from the roof of the school to get a bird's-eye view of the area that potentially could be used for a garden. During their discussion, Abby asked the children if they would like to have more flowers and plants to observe outside the classroom. The response was an enthusiastic yes. At that point, the children decided the courtyard was a perfect place for a garden and they were ready to decide exactly where it could be planted.

Once the children were invested in the plan of making a garden, Phase One work began. The children began to represent what they already knew about plants and gardens with drawings, paintings, modeling clay, and other materials. As a group, the class created a web to record prior experiences and ideas the children generated. Abby turned the dramatic play area into a garden center. She brought books on gardens and plants, seed and plant catalogs, and gardening tools into the classroom. As a group the class began to gain some common knowledge on gardening and plants and decided the garden was going to be a flower garden. The children also decided they should make a garden that would be a good habitat for the birds they had been feeding all winter. The enthusiasm was building and the children were eager to get their hands in the dirt. As they planned, the children began to wonder and ask questions about gardening, seeds, and plants. It became obvious that they needed more information to make a garden. As a class they decided to investigate the following questions:

- Where do seeds come from? How do they grow?
- Why do plants have flowers? Why do plants have different flowers and why do they smell pretty? Why do plants have leaves?

- What plants will be good for feeding the birds?
- What kinds of birds come to our garden? What do they need in their habitat?

Once they decided which questions to explore, Abby asked each child individually which question he was most interested in investigating. This is how the research groups were created. Abby knew she wanted the children to visit a nursery and have an opportunity to ask questions of a gardening expert. One of the kindergarten parents had a small gardening business with a greenhouse and several gardens, so Abby planned a field trip to Green Acres Garden Greenhouse. In preparation for the field trip, Abby went to the greenhouse to meet with the parent, plan the schedule, and discuss how the children could have hands-on experiences, collect their data, and record the information. In preparation for the trip, the teaching assistant, parent helpers, and Abby worked with groups of children to prepare questions to ask the gardening expert.

The trip to Green Acres Greenhouse was a fantastic experience and gave the children lots of information. Each child had a clipboard to sketch and record measurements, quantities, and other information. Some children did rubbings of flowers and leaves; some measured the garden and the rows with string and adding machine tape. The children counted types of pots and tools and made charts showing the different types of flowers, their colors, their sizes, and how much sun they needed. The information the children collected was very impressive.

For the next four weeks, the Phase Two fieldwork of planning, preparing, and planting the garden took place. The children started some seeds inside the classroom to be transplanted at a later date. All the children participated in digging the area for the flower garden and amending and working the soil to make it ready for planting seeds. The decisions about what plants to grow became focused on plants that would be good for birds. With support, a group of children gathered information on plants that would attract birds. Another group was very curious about the sprouting of seeds. They planted seeds in clear plastic cups and zip-top bags so the children could observe how they grew. Other children dissected different kinds of flowers to see what was inside. They examined and compared the many different kinds of seeds as they planted the garden. Several children decided to keep track of the birds that visited the bird feeders in the courtyard to determine what kinds of flowers would provide the food they needed. The children decided they should call the garden the Bird Garden.

Finally, they had the garden planted with seeds, seedlings, and some annuals from the greenhouse that were already blooming. The children were bursting with excitement and pride. It was time to move into Phase Three and share the garden and all they had learned. The class planned a Bird Garden Fair to celebrate. Abby displayed the children's work from the very beginning of the project to the end. The children made invitations, signs, charts, graphs, drawings, and paintings to represent the story of their project.

On the day of the fair, the children greeted the visitors and took them on guided tours around the classroom and then outside into the garden. At the end of the project Abby was reminded of the tremendous amount of learning that had taken place during the garden project. Project work has had a profound impact on her teaching.

Outdoor Center Time Activities

Water Play

A real change from the regular routine of center time in the classroom is to set up center time activities outdoors. Water play is a treat as an outdoor center. We bring our water table outdoors and fill it with lots of warm, soapy water. Large tubs or dishpans work too. We provide measuring cups, spoons, different-sized containers, turkey basters, tubing, rotary beaters, and so on. The children love washing the dolls in the water table with small hand brushes, sponges cut in half, baby washcloths, and bars of soap. The children love to clean the babies and make tons of soapsuds.

Another water activity is to fill a bucket or dishwashing basin with very thick soapy water and have all kinds of bubble-blowing equipment available. Obviously the standard bubble wands (those small plastic circles with handles) are great, but we like to add other, more unusual items as well. We use plastic strawberry baskets, pipe cleaners twisted in different shapes, and a very large thick string tied to a dowel that the children can dunk in the solution and then spread out and blow into or on a windy day just let the wind blow the bubbles. Straws are fun for the children to blow into the bubble bucket or dishpan so that they can make mountains of bubbles (keep enough straws nearby for each child to have her own). Scholastic has a great book titled *Pop! A Book About Bubbles*, by Kimberly Brubaker Bradley (2003), that is part of its Read and Let's Find Out series.

Sink or Float

Sometimes during water play, we like to give the children a variety of objects that sink and float. This is a good activity to have children work in pairs. We begin by providing many different objects and asking the children to just experiment with these things to see which sink and which float. We use objects like little boats so children can really play a while. The first time children use any new materials, they need time to explore. After they have had free play, they will be ready to try the planned activities.

The next time the children use the water table, they are ready for a more structured activity. We give them an assortment of ten different objects, some that float and some that don't. We ask them to take one object at a time and predict if it will sink or float, put it in the water, and then record their findings. We give each team a clipboard and a record sheet on which to write and draw the results of their experiment.

Painting

Painting outdoors is always a hit! Debra brings out easels and hangs paper on them or hangs up paper from a large roll on a fence with clothespins. She has also attached it to the side of a building with some duct tape. Instead of using only brushes, you can have some spray bottles with very watered-down paint, feather dusters, rollers, sponges, squares of carpet, and so on. In fact, these are the things that make great "pretty paper," which we use in our scenery for the end-of-the-year celebration or Mother's Day. A very effective technique is to have the children paint the paper a solid color, let it dry, and the next day use all the unusual painting items to layer colors and textures over the solid. We create some papers in the blue family, some in the orange family, some in the yellow, and so on. This way when we create huge pieces of scenery for a sun, tree, people, and animals, we have different colors for different items. This technique can also be used to create murals and bulletin boards. These painting activities are primarily for the process and not the product, so we step back and let the children enjoy the unusual painting experiences.

Another outdoor painting experience we have tried is "painting the school." We bring out paintbrushes (preferably the old ones) with cans of water and let the children "paint" up and down the sides of the school building. We also sometimes let them draw on the building with large sidewalk chalk. We hose it all off or let the rain wash it off. By the way, we recommend giving a heads-up to the custodian.

More Outdoor Activities

A battery-operated tape or CD player is great for small groups of children to listen to stories and music in a quiet, shady spot. Put down a blanket and if possible some older pillows and you have a relaxing area.

Lego toys on a table under a tree or in a shaded area is a favorite of the construction enthusiasts. A spot where the children can dig in the dirt or sand is another good outdoor center activity for a group. Small hand shovels and trucks work fine as well as some of the standard sand toys. Any hole children dig can easily be filled in at cleanup time. Again, we recommend informing the custodian.

Figure 10–1. Scott's drawing of the playground

Often we will use clipboards and go outside to sketch flowers, trees, or even the playground. This can be part of a theme or project or just an activity to help the children take a closer look. By sketching or representing these things, children learn to look carefully and notice much more.

The children can carry large hollow-core blocks outdoors to create imaginative play structures such as caves, castles, ships, and other buildings. An old flat-bottom rowboat can make a great outdoor prop for the spring season. It will not last forever on your playground, but it will add to the imaginative play during this special outdoor time. Let your imagination rule as you add any other props to this area for the children to pretend and play with. Things like life preservers, old camping equipment, a small pup tent, dishes, and more will further develop elaborate play.

For a special day, we may want to have a "fun in the sun day" or a beach day. On this day, sprinklers, a few small plastic pools, the bubble and water tables, and any other water play activity would be a big hit. Parents can apply sunscreen at home before school. Each child brings a large towel to school so he can lie down to warm up after he gets wet. It is nice to add some simple refreshments such as watermelon, juice, popcorn, or freezer pops. Some schools are better equipped and encourage this type of outdoor play. Access to water and shaded areas, the proximity of an outdoor play area to the classroom, and storage space all have an impact on our outdoor play. Whatever we do, the children are thrilled to be outside. If you live in a part of the world with a warm climate all year, this may be the routine. But as we mentioned earlier, in the Northeast it is a celebration to be outdoors again with the children.

Read-Alouds for Experienced Listeners

In May we share some of our favorite stories and authors and read books that have more text and may need to be read over a few days. The children are older now and experienced at listening to us read aloud. They are ready for longer and more complex stories. One of the children's favorites at this time of year is *The Bear That Heard Crying,* by Natalie Kinsey-Warnock and Helen Kinsey (1993). This story is based on a true tale that took place two hundred years ago. It is about a little girl who gets lost in the woods and encounters a bear that she thinks is a big black dog. The bear helps her until the rescue party finds her. When we read this book (over two days), the children are motionless and wide-eyed, waiting to find out what will happen to Sarah. The ending is such a relief that we can feel the tension lift as we read the last pages. The children also love that Sarah thought the bear was a dog and, of course, they know the truth.

The Summer of Stanley, by Natalie Kinsey-Warnock (1997) is also based on a true story, but the time period is World War II. Stanley is a pet goat who is forever doing destructive things. Nevertheless, Tyler loves him. Dad is off in Europe fighting in the war and Mom gets unexpectedly called away. Sister Molly is left in charge until Mom returns. Tyler takes Stanley and goes fishing. Tyler gets hot and decides to go for a swim. The stream is running swiftly and Tyler gets in big trouble. Molly and Stanley come to his aid but not until there is much tension and drama over Tyler's rescue. The ending is exciting as well as touching.

Good Books for Late-Spring Read-Alouds
DiTerlizzi, T. 2001. *Ted.* New York: Simon and Schuster Books for Young Readers.
Kinsey-Warnock, N. 1997. *The Summer of Stanley.* New York: Dutton.
Kinsey-Warnock, N., and H. Kinsey. 1993. *The Bear That Heard Crying.* New York: Dutton.
MacLachlan, P. 1994. *All the Places to Love.* New York: HarperCollins.

Munsch, R. 2003. *Lighthouse, A Story of Remembrance*. New York: Greenwillow Books.

Pinkney, A. 1998. *Duke Ellington*. New York: Hyperion Books for Children.

Stevens, J. 1995. *Tops and Bottoms*. New York: Harcourt Brace.

Vaughan, M. 1999. *Abbie Against the Storm*. Hillsboro, OR: Beyond Words.

Mother's Day Celebration

When Mother's Day comes in May, it is a wonderful opportunity to recognize our kindergartners' moms. We love to have our moms come to school and pamper them a bit. Sometimes there is a child who does not reside with her mom or whose mom has died or is away on business. Therefore, the invitation to the Mother's Day event includes grandmas, aunts, sisters, and close family friends. Among all these family members, there usually is someone special in the life of that child who can attend. And if there isn't, we make sure a teacher, librarian, principal, or other person will be there for that student.

About two weeks prior to Mother's Day we have a class meeting and discuss this event. We ask the children to choose their favorite songs and dances to do with their moms. We often read a poem or book. Two Mother's Day books that the children and moms have enjoyed are *What Moms Can't Do*, by Douglas Wood (2001), and *Hazel's Amazing Mother* (1985), by Rosemary Wells.

Some things the children can make for this special event are table decorations, place mats, and name cards. The children can work on small books about their mothers a week or two before. It's reasonable to have them complete a page a day. We like to provide a structure for the books.

Page 1: Draw a picture of your mom and write about a physical characteristic. Some examples are "My mom has blue eyes," "My mom is beautiful," and "My mom has red hair."

Page 2: Write about something you like to do with your mom and draw a picture of it. Some examples are "My mom and I play games," "We plant a garden," and "My mom reads to me."

Page 3: Complete this sentence: I love my mom because . . .

Page 4: Write "Happy Mother's Day" and the date.

The children can read these books to their moms or grandmas at the table while enjoying refreshments. Or depending on space, half of the class can have refreshments while the other children read their books aloud to their moms. This can provide some good laughs and some tears of joy.

Refreshments are one of the nicest ways we can make the moms feel pampered. We do a reception with small muffins, quartered bagels, tea breads, and

Figure 10–2. Sean reads his book at the Mother's Day celebration.

fruit. Debra begins baking about a week ahead so that there are many homemade treats. Bonnie asks the dads to contribute some culinary delights (but graciously accepts whatever she gets). We provide juice, milk, and water. Butter, jelly, and cream cheese are available for the muffins and bagels. We set it out with care, using amenities such as a tablecloth, flowers, serving bowls and baskets, and small spreading knives. It is all done in a spirit of gratitude and the moms are very appreciative. We recruit someone to help put out food, pour juice, and clean up. This way, we can visit more with the moms and children and not be quite so frantic.

An Artist Theme

Bonnie has often done a theme on famous artists in May. There are some wonderful books about the lives of famous artists like Monet, Picasso, Matisse, and Van Gogh. One series by Mike Venezia has interesting information about the artists as well as examples of their art. The texts are a bit too lengthy, so Bonnie paraphrases the information as she shows the students the pictures. Another series by Mila Boutan has limited text, great information, and beautiful illustrations. She has written books about Monet, Van Gogh, Cezanne, Degas, Gaugin, Matisse, Picasso, and Renoir. After reading about a particular artist and looking at samples of his work, the children may try to replicate his style.

145

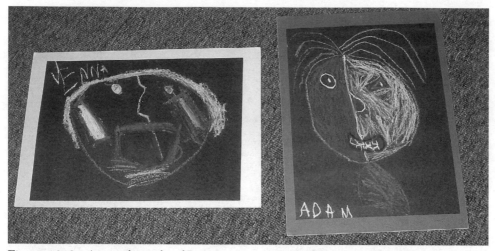

Figure 10–3. Art in the style of Picasso

A favorite story is *Camille and the Sunflowers,* by Laurence Anholt (1994). It is a very moving story about a young boy's experience when Vincent van Gogh moves to his town. Another resource that is wonderful to use when teaching children about different types of art and artists is *A Child's Book of Art,* by Lucy Micklethwait (1993).

Books About Art

Anholt, L. 1994. *Camille and the Sunflowers.* Hauppauge, NY: Barron's.
Boutan, M. 1996. *Monet Art Activity Pack.* San Francisco: Chronicle Books.
Lepscky, I. 1984. *Pablo Picasso.* New York: Trumpet Club.
Maynard, B. 1997. *Incredible Ned.* New York: G. P. Putnam's Sons.
Micklethwait, L. 1993. *A Child's Book of Art.* New York: Dorling Kindersley.
Moon, N. 1994. *Lucy's Picture.* New York: Puffin.
Venezia, M. 1993. *Monet.* Chicago: Children's.
West, A. 1996. *Jamaica Louise James.* Cambridge, MA: Candlewick.
Lionni, L. 1991. *Matthew's Dream.* NewYork: Alfred A. Knopf.

A wonderful way to spend time with our colleagues, families, or friends is to visit art museums to learn more about the artists. We are fortunate to have several museums in our area. In Amherst, Massachusetts, we have visited the Eric Carle Museum and we have also done a bus trip to the Metropolitan Museum of Art in New York City to view and discuss Caldecott art. The gift shops are excellent resources for purchasing postcards, prints, games, and books to be used in the classroom. Sometimes it is possible to have local artists come to the classroom to share their work or to obtain funding to have artists work with the children over a period of time.

Final Assessment

Since we end our school year in June, there is a big push early in May to finish the final round of assessments. Depending on the number of students we have and how much help we receive from other staff members, it might be necessary to begin in April. We feel a good rule of thumb is to try to finish all the assessments about one month before the last day of school. This gives us plenty of time to complete the progress reports and all the end-of-the-year forms that need to be filed in various places.

Using the same record forms that we have used since the start of school, we continue with each child where we left off in January. Most of the students identify upper- and lowercase letters and most consonant sounds by May. We also ask each child to write the same five words that we assessed in October and January to determine growth in sound spelling. By this time, many children will use some vowels or even some traditional spellings. We also have a list of twenty to twenty-four sight words that the children are expected to read by the end of kindergarten or early first grade. Most children do this successfully because we have these words all around the room and have used the words in many ways, such as in our daily messages and on song charts.

We have also focused on two words from this list each week starting in January and added them to a list in the classroom. The Early Literacy Profile also includes a sentence dictation segment. We dictate two very basic sentences and score them for spelling, spacing, capitalization, and punctuation. Most of the writing we do in kindergarten is done in a cooperative and collaborative way, so asking a child to write a sentence or two without help can be frustrating for the child and the teacher! We try to present these tasks in a stress-free manner and tell the children, "All the kindergartners are doing this. Just do your best."

We do the final running records to determine each child's reading level as she leaves kindergarten. Lastly, we assess math skills not previously mastered on the assessment.

Currently, we are comfortable with the assessments our districts are using, but over the years we each have been expected to use assessment tools that we weren't completely comfortable with. Our advice is to administer them in a gentle way and then work with colleagues to inform your principal and district administrators about more developmentally appropriate assessments. Take the time to research the options, talk to colleagues in other districts, and advocate for alternatives that are in line with district and state standards. Reform in schools can be painfully slow—especially when you are the one trying to do the reforming.

We recommend starting with your colleagues at the primary grades in your school and district. Perhaps forming a study group where members read and discuss professional books and articles would be a good way to begin. Consult professional organizations to see what they recommend. One book we have found useful is *Learning to Read and Write: Developmentally Appropriate Practices for Young Children*, by Neuman, Copple, and Bredekamp (2000). This book bridges the work done in literacy and early childhood education and provides specific examples of how to teach literacy in a developmentally appropriate way. A second step could be speaking to the assistant superintendent for instruction and planning speakers and inservice that support your goals. We prefer some ongoing support and not just one-time keynote speakers. It is more helpful to work with knowledgeable people who will sit down and work with teachers over time, go into classrooms, do demonstration lessons, and give teachers opportunities to discuss, share, and question.

Summary

Completing another round of assessment records with each child is a big job. Since these are the final assessments administered in kindergarten, it feels very satisfying to have them completed and to see the growth most children have made in the school year. It also feels wonderful to have May's warm, sunny days. It is a treat to spend time outdoors on the playground, planting or participating in outdoor center time activities.

After our Mother's Day celebration, we reflect on the fond feelings we have for the children and their families. There is a special bond with the parents who helped a great deal and families with older siblings whom we taught in previous years. Building these relationships is truly one of the most joyful parts of our job.

June and July

Coming Full Circle

June is bittersweet because we have worked, played, laughed, and shared so much and now it is time to plan for the end of the school year. This juxtaposition creates joy, sadness, and some stress! It is as important to plan for the closing of the school year as it is to plan for the opening. One of our goals for ending the year is to help the children reflect on their time in kindergarten. We plan different ways to help them share this information. Holding a closing celebration performance allows the parents and extended families of the children to feel the happiness and see the growth the children have made throughout the year. In the teaching profession we are fortunate to have a clear beginning and ending. This ending month allows us to bring closure for the children and for ourselves. In this chapter, we elaborate on suggestions for Father's Day, end-of-the-year projects, and culminating activities. It is also time to finish all the reports and paperwork, clean out, organize, and pack up.

Father's Day Celebration

Unlike many school districts, we are still in session for Father's Day. We have a simple celebration for dads and invite them to school. Similar to Mother's Day, this event is for dads, grandfathers, uncles, big brothers, or close family friends. In today's world, where 50 percent of marriages end in divorce and many of our children are living in single-parent households or with a stepparent or grandparent, the invitations to our special events are inclusive. We think there is value in having such parent celebrations and we do not want to eliminate them. Therefore, we try to be sensitive and find a way to make all children feel included.

We call this event Donuts with Dad. This makes it pretty clear that it will not be an elaborate reception or event. In fact, most dads seem to appreciate a briefer time period and a less formal celebration. To accommodate busy work schedules, it is helpful to have the dads come right at the start of our school day. Similar to Mother's Day, we ask the children in advance at the morning meeting what they would like to sing with their dads.

Before the day of our celebration, we ask each child to draw a picture of her dad with a short story under it. We have them mounted colorfully and on display when the dads arrive. In addition, Bonnie has dads donate unwanted ties before Thanksgiving to be used for a huge turkey tail on a bulletin board. She has the children paint turkeys to hang around the big turkey with the tail made of ties. When Father's Day rolls around, she gets the ties out of the closet and has each child select a recycled tie and wrap it for his dad. You know what they say: one man's trash is another man's treasure. Bonnie even has an endless supply of U.S. maps scrounged from a local company that the children use as wrapping paper.

Debra has her children make ties for their dads from oak tag colored with bright markers, glitter pens, and pictures of themselves stuck to the center. After the school photos are taken, we receive several small photos of each child. They come in handy for projects like this one.

We like to have dads join the children for a sing-along, so we display the songs on charts. Sometimes we read some poems or a story to either kick off or end the event. A good way to organize the time is to divide into three groups. One group can eat donuts or bagels, another can build with blocks and Lego toys, and a third group can do a project. We like to make the project something for the dads. One project we have enjoyed is covering rocks about the size of a fist with small squares of brightly colored tissue papers for each dad. We attach and layer the tissue squares with Mod Podge sealer or watered-down glue. They can be used as a paper weight or displayed as a work of art. The time frame for the festivities is about one hour. From our experience, the dads leave feeling happy to be remembered and the children are thrilled they got to sing and play with their dads or special guests.

Thank You and Good-Bye

June is the time to thank the volunteers for all their hard work. Sometimes we have a reception after school without children so we can visit and have light refreshments together to say thank you. Other times we may send a small gift and a heartfelt thank-you card home to each volunteer. We are so grateful for all of their help and could never give the children so much individual and small-group attention without them. They are an integral part of a developmentally appropriate kindergarten.

We also like to thank the people who work at school and help us. We make cards for the secretaries, custodians, and aides, who do so much. We often invite

Figure 11–1. Book buddies say good-bye.

the principal to read us a story at the end of the year to say our good-byes until September.

Some years we pair up with a class of older students and have book buddies. We get together each week throughout the year and read together, write together, and even build and draw and play games. The children become very fond of each other and it is often difficult to say good-bye in June. We usually go to the playground and have ice-cream sundaes or freezer pops on our last day together.

Class Reflections

At a June morning meeting we guide our children to reflect upon their year by telling them that the children who are coming to school next year want to know about kindergarten. We ask the seasoned kindergartners if they have some advice,

151

Figure 11–2. Reflections on the kindergarten year, by Madison

feelings, predictions, or statements to share with the new kindergartners. Each child can make a page for a class book to be shared with next year's students on the first day of school. We also take the children's reflections and weave them into our last newsletter or closing letter. It is remarkable how sensitive and poignant their combined thoughts are in a final communication.

Another way to help the children reflect on the year is to make small books. Some pages we have included are "This is my teacher," "This is my school," "These are my friends," and "Some things I liked learning about are. . . ." At the end of the books we provide a couple of blank pages for the children to collect each other's autographs. It is always very exciting for the children to buzz around the classroom and ask each other for signatures.

Closing Celebration

From past experience we have learned that it is best to have the closing celebration a few weeks before the end of school. If we wait until the last week, then we are not relaxed and enjoying the children as the year draws to a close. A bit of tension does exist before the show takes place, so it is preferable to end the year with calm, predictable, and joyful activities. Parents are probably grateful not to have all their commitments at the end of the school year, particularly if they have a few children.

At Bonnie's school, kindergartners don't do an end-of-the-year program. She brings closure to the year with a picnic at her home. She invites the kindergartners and their families to her home on a Saturday in June shortly before school ends for the year. Bonnie lives in an old farmhouse with a big barn, a pond, and lots of land, so it is the perfect spot for a big picnic. The children bring nets to scoop tadpoles, visit the horses nearby, tour the gardens and barn, and generally learn about country life.

Figure 11–3. Picnic at Bonnie's farm

Recordkeeping

Before the school year is over we need to sort and file the assessment records we have gathered on each child. All of the formal and informal assessment pieces make for a complete record of each child's growth and achievement for the first-grade teachers to review and use. We group all of the language assessment records in a reading folder. We turn those folders over to the reading department, who later sorts them by the new first-grade classes. Writing samples are saved in a cumulative writing folder that begins in kindergarten and moves with the child through fifth grade. We have had many students come back to us to say they couldn't believe what they wrote in kindergarten! Debra also has a math assessment to be filed in a math folder that follows the child through grade 5. Bonnie has a slightly different form that summarizes the child's progress in all areas that she places in the child's cumulative folder and copies for the first-grade teacher. Lastly, we add a photo to each child's official cumulative folder along with his progress reports.

Packing Up

The second biggest job after setting up the classroom each school year is packing it away. In our schools we have to completely pack up the room for a thorough cleaning and because the school space is used by other programs in the summer. Although this is a huge job, we find this is a good way for us to reflect upon the year and make decisions about what to keep and what to toss. Kindergarten teachers are savers, pack rats, and treasure seekers. There are very few professions where someone arrives in a car at your door saying, "I saved these all winter for you," and falling out of her car are stacks of wooden clementine boxes.

As we pack up we try to determine whether materials and supplies were well used. If not, then it is time to give them away. There are many other organizations that are grateful to receive our unwanted classroom items. Furniture, puzzles, yellowed or inappropriately lined paper, extra egg cartons, paper towel rolls, pine cones, and any other items that are still in decent condition might be used by nursery schools, day care centers, and after-school programs.

One year at Debra's school, teachers held a gigantic garage sale. During a designated week at the end of the year, teachers were told to place any unwanted items outside their classrooms. This meant anything—books, paper, art supplies, puzzles, furniture, the kitchen sink! It was an enormous treasure hunt. Most teachers cleared out many unwanted items but in turn filled any empty space with their new finds. It would probably be wise to hold this tag sale at the end of every school year to prevent teachers from accumulating so much.

At this time of the year, empty paper boxes near the photocopy machine become coveted items. We have found it worthwhile to pack carefully and group items together according to their place in the room. If the forms and paperwork are completed a few weeks before the end of the year, then this is possible. Otherwise the packing becomes random and harried, and the setting up in August and September is that much harder.

Professional Growth

In our school districts, inservice courses are offered during the summer months. In Debra's district it is a joke around June to ask which boot camp your colleagues are attending. Seriously, we are fortunate to be given so many professional choices within our districts and in our area.

Our registration and participation in professional growth are guided in two ways. There are initiatives that our school districts designate as priorities. These are areas in which the school district hopes to educate all teachers. Also, during our formal evaluations with our administrators, we make commitments to study and improve our understanding in an area and to attend related training. In Debra's district there has been much focus and attention on better developing and using the writers workshop approach in the classroom. When the writers workshop course was initially offered, Debra was hesitant and it was not her first choice of study for her growth and development as a kindergarten teacher. But this initiative and follow-up was an important priority in her district. Because of the great instructors and their extensive knowledge and experience, it has become a personal goal for Debra to effectively use writers workshop as part of her writing program.

Bonnie jokes that she should be awarded numerous honorary degrees for being married to her husband, Sean, for more than twenty-five years. He is chair of the reading department at the University at Albany and a consultant to many school districts that are rethinking their literacy programs. Many of their conversations at home are related to education and she is continually exposed to research and best practices in teaching literacy.

We choose some workshops and courses because they address personal goals we have created for ourselves. Perhaps we read a book during the school year or took a workshop that sparked an interest or passion. For Debra, studying more about the project approach was such a decision. She had read *Engaging Children's Minds*, by Dr. Lilian Katz and Dr. Sylvia Chard (1989), and decided to take a course on the project approach one summer. It turned out to be extremely meaningful and was the type of work she wanted to have her children doing during the school year. Her colleagues became interested in what she had learned and then the school district encouraged more teachers to study and implement the project approach. So what began as a personal goal became part of a districtwide inservice.

The best professional development instills passion and creates commitment that is contagious. This commitment and our excitement become evident to our kindergartners, parents, colleagues, and administrators.

This is also the time to choose some professional books along with great books that are completely unrelated to education. Now all we need is some quiet time in a comfortable and cool place.

Throughout the year, but mostly in summer, Bonnie does workshops and presents at conferences around the country. Debra also leads study groups and workshops for teachers in our area. We find that preparing to teach the teachers strengthens our knowledge and understanding of kindergarten issues and practices. We need to reflect carefully on our beliefs anytime we set out to articulate our philosophies and practices to our colleagues.

Summary

June is the time we want to thank our parent volunteers. Our school year was enriched and more productive because of their support and expertise.

We also want to show our appreciation to our book buddies for the kindness and patience they showed our kindergartners. A simple celebration outdoors gives the buddies a time to say their good-byes. Additionally, we thank all our support staff who helped us during the year. We are careful to remember the custodian who came to our rescue in many emergencies. Debra remembers the time the plug was "accidentally" pulled out of the water table. Water was gushing out of the drain and onto the floor!

Writing reports and the final organization of all the folders and papers is a big job. When it is complete, we breathe a big sign of relief.

This is also the time of year when the children are speaking and writing about their reflections of kindergarten. We are showered with thank-you notes and love notes from the children as they leave for the summer. Our love of kindergarten children and teaching kindergarten is reinforced.

Epilogue

As the end of the school year approaches, we are extremely busy. We are filing final reports and assessments, having numerous first-grade placement meetings, and making decisions about what to save and what to give away or toss. There are many details to consider as we bring closure to the school year.

And then the final day of school arrives. Many hugs, good-byes, and some tears are exchanged. Saying good-bye can be emotional, especially when we have taught several children in a family and this is the last child to attend kindergarten. There is much sentiment and emotion packed into the last week and especially the final day.

The children leave and there is silence. It is always a bit eerie returning to the bare and empty classroom. In the stillness we are grateful to have time to ponder the year past. We remember the day we had apples for snack and Anthony lost his tooth while eating his apple and we searched all the apple cores in the trashcan to find his tooth. We recall the day Melissa proudly announced, "I can read all of *Brown Bear* without even looking at the words!" We worry about how some children will fare as they head on to first grade or what the summer will bring for some of the families who are at risk.

There have been many successes and plenty of challenges along the way. Through it all our sense of humor and the humor of the children have been so important. How fortunate we are to be surrounded each day by kindergarten wit. No matter how many times we hear the joke about the chicken crossing the road, we still have to chuckle. Relating the stories and jokes of the day to our families in the evening doesn't pack the same punch it did in the classroom. Oh well— guess you had to be there.

The adjustment from the hectic life of our school routines to the relaxed pace of summer will take some time. We usually begin this transition by making a list of all the projects around the house we have put off for months. We attack these projects for the first week or so of vacation as an outlet for our extra energy. Soon we ease into the summer schedule and actually relax and begin reading the piles of books we have accumulated and begin working for hours in our gardens. We can read late into the night or maybe even linger over breakfast.

Last summer was a bit different. We didn't have much time to linger because we were hard at work on this book. Along with the hard work came the opportunity to clarify our thoughts about early childhood education and articulate our beliefs and passions. It was comforting to both of us that we do have strong convictions and that our continued education and experience have made us more capable and compassionate teachers. As we finish this book, we wonder where we have found the extra time and energy, considering what we do each day in our classrooms and our homes. We hope we have been able to share our love of teaching and our commitment to kindergartners. Teaching kindergarten can be demanding and sometimes even exhausting work. But seeing the children enter our classrooms full of enthusiasm and wonder, we are reminded that we get back much more than we give.

We thank you, the reader, for joining us on our journey through a year in kindergarten. And may you find joy and fulfillment as you work with your kindergartners each day.

Appendix

Alphabet Books

Carter, D. A. 1994. *Alpha Bugs*. New York: Little Simon.

Bayer, J. 1992. *A My Name Is Alice*. New York: Puffin.

Ehlert, L. 1989. *Eating the Alphabet*. San Diego: Harcourt Brace.

Horenstein, H. 1999. *Arf! Beg! and Catch!* New York: Scholastic.

Lobel, A. 1981. *On Market Street*. New York: Scholastic.

———. 1990. *Alison's Zinnia*. New York: Greenwillow.

Martin, B. J. 1989. *Chicka Chicka Boom Boom*. New York: Scholastic.

Pelletier, D. 1996. *The Graphic Alphabet*. New York: Scholastic.

Rankin, L. 1992. *The Handmade Alphabet*. New York: Dial Books for Young Readers.

Seeley, L. 1990. *The Book of Shadowboxes*. Atlanta: Peachtree Publishers.

Shannon, G. 1996. *Tomorrow's Alphabet*. New York: William Morrow.

Van Allsburg, C. 1987. *The Z Was Zapped*. Boston: Houghton Mifflin.

Walton, R. 1998. *So Many Bunnies*. New York: William Morrow.

Wood, A. 2001. *Alphabet Adventure*. New York: Blue Sky.

———. 2003. *Alphabet Mystery*. New York: Blue Sky.

Social Studies Books

Bellamy, F. 2000. *The Pledge of Allegiance*. New York: Scholastic.

Brown, T. 1984. *Someone Special, Just Like You*. New York: Henry Holt and Company.

Chinn, K., and C. Van Wright. 1997. *Sam and the Lucky Money*. New York: Lee and Low Books.

Fox, M. 1997. *Whoever You Are*. New York: Harcourt, Brace, and Company.

Haan, A. 2003. *I Call My Hand Gentle*. New York: Penguin Books.

Intrater, R. 1995. *Two Eyes, a Nose, and a Mouth*. New York: Scholastic.

Marzolla, J. 1993. *Happy Birthday Martin Luther King*. New York: Scholastic.

Morris, A. 1989a. *Hats, Hats, Hats*. New York: Scholastic.

———. 1989b. *Bread, Bread, Bread*. New York: HarperCollins.

———. 1990. *Loving*. New York: HarperCollins.

———. 1992. *Houses and Homes*. New York: HarperCollins.

———. 1995. *Shoes, Shoes, Shoes*. New York: Lothrop, Lee, & Shepard.

———. 1998. *Work*. New York: Lothrop, Lee, & Shepard.

———. 1999. *Teamwork*. New York: Lothrop, Lee, & Shepard.

———. 2000. *Families*. New York: HarperCollins.

Rappaport, D. 2001. *Martin's Big Words*. New York: Hyperion Books for Children.

Reid, M. 1997. *A String of Beads*. New York: Dutton Children's.

Tarpley, N. 1998. *I Love My Hair!* Boston: Little, Brown.

Waters, K. 1990. *Lion Dancer, Ernie Wan's Chinese New Year*. New York: Scholastic.

Wells, R. 1985. *Hazel's Amazing Mother*. New York: Dial Books for Young Readers.

Wood, D. 2001. *What Mother's Can't Do*. New York: Simon & Schuster Books for Young Readers.

Science Books

Asch, F. 1994. *The Earth and I*. New York: Harcourt Brace.

Bunting, E. 1997. *Sunflower House*. New York: Scholastic.

Carle, E. 1969. *The Hungry Caterpillar*. New York: Philomel.

Cowcher, H. 1990. *Antarctica*. New York: Scholastic.

Crews, D. 1978. *Freight Train*. Big book. New York: Greenwillow.

Editors of Klutz Press. 1996. *Shadow Games*. Palo Alto, CA: Klutz Press.

Ehlert, L. 1990. *Feathers for Lunch*. New York: Trumpet Club.

———. 1991. *Red Leaf, Yellow Leaf*. New York: Harcourt Brace Jovanovich.

———. 1993. *Nuts to You!* New York: Harcourt Brace.

———. 1995. *Snowballs*. New York: Harcourt Brace.

———. 2001. *Waiting for Wings*. New York: Harcourt.

Fleming, D. 1993. *In the Small, Small Pond*. New York: Scholastic.

George, L. B. 1995. *In the Snow: Who's Been Here?* New York: Greenwillow.

Gibbons, G. 1984. *The Seasons of Arnold's Apple Tree*. New York: Harcourt Brace Jovanovich.

———. 2000. *Apples*. New York: Scholastic.

Gore, S. 1989. *My Shadow*. New York: Doubleday.

Hall, Z. 1996. *The Apple Pie Tree*. New York: Scholastic.

Johnson, N. 1997. *A Field of Sunflowers*. New York: Scholastic.

Martin, B. J. 1992. *Brown Bear, Brown Bear, What Do You See?* New York: Holt, Rhinehart and Winston.

Mazzola, F. J. 1997. *Counting Is for the Birds*. New York: Scholastic.

Oppenheim, J. 1986. *Have You Seen Birds?* New York: Scholastic.

Robbins, K. 1998. *Autumn Leaves.* New York: Scholastic.

Ryder, J. 1982. *The Snail's Spell.* New York: Scholastic.

Rylant, C. 2000. *In November.* Orlando, FL: Harcourt, Inc.

Swinburne, S. 1999. *Guess Whose Shadow.* New York: Scholastic.

Walsh, E. S. 1989. *Mouse Paint.* New York: Harcourt Brace Jovanovich.

Warnock, N. 1993. *When Spring Comes.* New York: Dutton Children's.

Wellington, M. 2001. *Apple Farmer Annie.* New York: Dutton.

Wildsmith, B. 1974. *Squirrels.* New York: Scholastic.

————. 1980. *Animal Seasons.* Boston: Harcourt.

Simon, S. 2002. *Planets Around the Sun.* New York: Scholastic.

Math Books

Briggs, R. 1989. *Jim and the Beanstalk.* New York: Sandcastle.

Carter, D. A. 1992. *Over in the Meadow.* New York: Scholastic.

Lindbergh, R. 1987. *The Midnight Farm.* New York: Dial Books for Young Readers.

Mazzola, F. J. 1997. *Counting Is for the Birds.* New York: Scholastic.

McGrath, B. B. 1998. *The Cheerios Counting Book.* New York: Scholastic.

Peek, M. 1976. *The Balancing Act: A Counting Song.* New York: Clarion.

Reid, M. S. 1990. *The Button Box.* New York: Dutton Children's.

Rockwell, A. 2002. *100 School Days.* New York: HarperCollins.

Smith, M. 1995. *Counting Our Way to Maine.* New York: Orchard.

Swinburne, S. 1998. *Lots and Lots of Zebra Stripes.* Orlando, FL: Harcourt.

Walsh, E. 1991. *Mouse Count.* Orlando, FL: Harcourt.

Chant and Song Books

Adams, P. 1991. *There Was an Old Lady Who Swallowed a Fly.* Singapore: Child's Play.

Carle, E. 1993. *Today Is Monday.* New York: Scholastic.

Frazee, M. 1999. *Hush, Little Baby.* New York: Scholastic.

Goodhart, P. 1997. *Row, Row, Row Your Boat.* New York: Scholastic.

Gunson, C. 1995. *Over on the Farm.* New York: Scholastic.

Hale, S. 1990. *Mary Had a Little Lamb.* New York: Scholastic.

Hoberman, M. 1998. *Miss Mary Mack.* New York: Scholastic.

Hort, L. 2000. *The Seals on the Bus.* New York: Scholastic.

Hutchins, P. 2000. *Ten Red Apples.* New York: Scholastic.

Miller, P., and S. Greene. 1982. *We All Sing with the Same Voice.* New York: HarperCollins. (CD packaged with book)

Moffat, J. 1996. *Who Stole the Cookies?* New York: Scholastic.

Norworth, J. 1999. *Take Me Out to the Ballgame.* New York: Aladdin Paperbacks.

O'Brien, J. 2000. *The Farmer in the Dell.* New York: Scholastic.

Paxton, T. 1996. *Going to the Zoo.* New York: Morrow Junior.

Slaot, T. 1998. *There Was an Old Lady That Swallowed a Trout.* New York: Scholastic.

Taback, S. 1997. *There Was an Old Lady Who Swallowed a Fly.* New York: Viking.

———. 2003. *Joseph Had a Little Overcoat.* New York: Scholastic.

Tiegreen, A. 1991. *Anna Banana: 101 Jump Rope Rhymes.* New York: Scholastic.

Trapani, I. 1993. *The Itsy Bitsy Spider.* New York: Scholastic.

Weiss, D., and B. Thiele. 1995. *What a Wonderful World.* New York: Atheneum Books for Young Readers.

Westcott, N. B. 1980. *I Know an Old Lady That Swallowed a Fly.* Boston: Little, Brown.

———. 1987a. *Down by the Bay.* New York: Crown.

———. 1987b. *Peanut Butter and Jelly.* New York: Trumpet Club.

———. 1988. *The Lady with the Alligator Purse.* Boston: Little, Brown.

Whippo, W. 2000. *Little White Duck.* New York: Scholastic.

Wickstrom, S. K. 1988. *Wheels on the Bus.* New York: Troll.

Zemach, H., and M. Zemach. 1966. *Mommy, Buy Me a China Doll.* Toronto, ON: Collins.

Poetry and Finger Plays

Brown, M. 1980. *Finger Rhymes.* New York: EP Dutton.

———. 1985. *Hand Rhymes.* New York: EP Dutton.

———. 1987. *Play Rhymes.* New York: EP Dutton.

dePaola., T. 1985. *Mother Goose.* New York: G.P. Putnam's & Sons.

Katz. A. 2001. *Take Me Out of the Bathtub.* New York: Simon & Schuster, Children's Publishing Division.

———. 2003. *I'm Still Here in the Bathtub.* New York: Simon & Schuster, Children's Publishing Division.

Lansky, B. 2004. *Mary Had a Little Jam.* New York: Simon & Schuster.

Prelutsky, J. 1986. *Read-Aloud Rhymes for the Very Young.* New York: Alfred A. Knopf.

More Great Books

Cronin, D. 2003. *Diary of a Worm.* New York: HarperCollins.

Davis, K. 2003. *Who Hops?* Orlando: Harcourt Brace.

dePaola, T. 1975. *Strega Nona.* New York: Scholastic.

Fox, M. 1992. *Koala Lou.* New York: Trumpet Club.

———. 1994. *Tough Boris.* New York: Trumpet Club.

French, J. 2003. *Diary of a Wombat*. Boston: Houghton Mifflin.

Gilman, P. 1992. *Something from Nothing*. New York: Scholastic.

Kraus, L. 1971. *Leo the Late Bloomer*. New York: Scholastic.

Martin, N. 1995. *The Maestro Plays*. New York: Scholastic.

Masogmen, S. 2002. *When I Grow Up I Want to be Me*. New York: Scholastic.

Schmidt, K. 2003. *Hoptoad*. New York: Harcourt Brace.

Waddell, M. 1992. *Owl Babies*. Cambridge, MA: Candlewick Press.

Willems, M. 2003. *Don't Let the Pigeon Drive the Bus!* New York: Hyperion Books for Children.

Professional Books

Adams, M. J., B. Foorman, I. Lundberg, and T. Beeler. 1998. *Phonemic Awareness in Young Children*. Baltimore, MD: Paul H. Brookes.

Butler, D., and M. Clay. 1995. *Reading Begins at Home*. Portsmouth, NH: Heinemann.

Cambourne, B. 1989. *The Whole Story*. New York: Scholastic.

Clay, M. 1975. *What Did I Write?* Portsmouth, NH: Heinemann.

———. 1987. *Writing Begins at Home*. Portsmouth, NH: Heinemann.

———. 2002. *An Observation Survey of Early Literacy Achievement*. Portsmouth, NH: Heinemann.

Diffily, D., and C. Sassman. 2002. *Project-Based Learning with Young Children*. Portsmouth, NH: Heinemann.

Duckworth, E. 1987. *The Having of Wonderful Ideas and Other Essays on Teaching and Learning*. New York: T.C.

Fox, M. 2001. *Reading Magic*. New York: Harcourt.

Griss, S. 1998. *Minds in Motion: A Kinesthetic Approach to Teaching Elementary Curriculum*. Portsmouth, NH: Heinemann.

Gullo, D. F. 1990. "The Changing Family Context: Implications for the Development of All-day Kindergarten" *Young Children* 45(4): 35–39. EJ 409 110.

Helm, J., and L. Katz. 2001. *Young Investigators: The Project Approach in the Early Years*. New York: Teacher's College Press.

Hirsch, E. 1984. *The Block Book*. Washington, DC: NAEYC.

Holdaway, D. 1979. *The Foundations of Literacy*. Portsmouth, NH: Heinemann.

Katz, L. G., and S. C. Chard. 1997. *Engaging Children's Minds: The Project Approach*. Norwood, NJ: Ablex.

Kriete, R. 1999. *The Morning Meeting Book*. Greenfield, MA: Northeast Foundation for Children.

Lasky, L. 1980. *Art: Basic for Young Children*. Washington, DC: NAEYC.

Miller, D. 2002. *Reading with Meaning*. Portland, ME: Stenhouse.

Morrow, L. 1997. *The Literacy Center*. Portland, ME: Stenhouse.

Neuman, S. B., C. Copple, and S. Bredekamp. 2000. *Learning to Read and Write: Developmentally Appropriate Practices for Young Children*. Washington, DC: NAEYC.

Olsen, D., and Zigler, E. 1989. "An Assessment at the All-day Kindergarten Movement." *Early Childhood Research Quarterly* 4(2): 167–186. EJ 394 085.

Owocki, G. 1999. *Literacy Through Play*. Portsmouth, NH: Heinemann.

———. G. 2001. *Make Way for Literacy*. Portsmouth, NH: Heinemann.

Ray, K. W. 2004. *About the Authors*. Portsmouth, NH: Heinemann.

Peck, J. T., G. McCaig, and M. E. Sapp. 1988. *Kindergarten Policies: What Is Best for Children*. Washington, DC: NAEYC.

Strickland, D. S., and L. M. Morrow. 1989. *Emerging Literacy: Young Children Learn to Read and Write*. Newark, DE: International Reading Association.

Topal, C. W., and L. Gandini. 1999. *Beautiful Stuff!* Worcester, MA: Davis.

Walmsley, B. B., A. M. Camp, and S. A. Walmsley. 1992a. *Teaching Kindergarten: A Developmentally Appropriate Approach*. Portsmouth, NH: Heinemann.

———. 1992b. *Teaching Kindergarten: A Theme-Centered Curriculum*. Portsmouth, NH: Heinemann.

Walmsley, B. B., and S. Walmsley. 1998. *Teaching with Favorite Marc Brown Books*. New York: Scholastic.

Walmsley, S. A. 1994. *Children Exploring Their World*. Portsmouth, NH: Heinemann.

Walmsley, S. A., and B. B. Walmsley. 1996. *Kindergarten: Ready or Not? A Parent's Guide*. Portsmouth, NH: Heinemann.

Wells, G. 1985. *Language Development in the Preschool Years*. Cambridge, UK: Cambridge University Press.

Music CDs

Allard, P. and E. Allard. 2002. *Sing It! Say It! Stamp It! Sway It!* Worcester, MA: 80 to Z Music.

Amidon, M. A. 1992. *Teaching Kindergarten*. Portsmouth, NH: Heinemann.

The Amidons. 1984. *Things Are Going My Way*.

———. 1990. *Songs for the Earth*.

———. 1993. *I'll Never Forget*.

Dr. Jean. 1998. *Dr. Jean and Friends*. Tampa, FL: Progressive Music.

———. 1999. *Keep on Singing and Dancing*. Tampa, FL: Progressive Music.

———. 2000. *Sing to Learn*. Tampa, FL: Progressive Music.

———. 2001a. Dr. Jean Sings Silly Songs. Tampa, FL: Progressive Music.

———. 2001b. *Is Everybody Happy?* Tampa, FL: Progressive Music.

Grammer, R. 1983. *Can You Sound Just Like Me?* Brewerton, NY: Red Note Records.

———. 1986. *Teaching Peace*. Brewerton, NY: Red Note Records.

———. 1991. *Down the Do-Re-Mi*. NY: Red Note Records.

———. 1991. *Favorite Sing-A-Long Songs*. Brewerton, NY: Red Note Records.

———. 1995. *Hello World*. Brewerton, NY: Red Note Records.

Greg and Steve. 1983. *We All Live Together*, vol. 1. Cypress, CA: Youngheart Music.

———. 1987a. *We All Live Together*, vol. 2. Cypress, CA: Youngheart Music.

———. 1987b. *Kids in Motion*. Cypress, CA: Youngheart Music.

———. 1997. *Big Fun*. Cypress, CA: Youngheart Music.

———. 2000. *Kids in Action*. Cypress, CA: Youngheart Music.

Jenkins, E. 1996. *Songs Children Love to Sing*. Washington, DC: Smithsonian Folkways Recording.

Miller, P., and S. Greene. 1982. *We All Sing with the Same Voice*. New York: HarperCollins.

New England Dancing Masters. 1991. *Jump Jim Joe: Great Singing Games for Children*. Brattleboro, VT: New England Dancing Masters.

———. 2000. *Down in the Valley*. Book and CD. Brattleboro, VT: New England Dancing Masters.

West, S. 1999. *Blue Sky City*. Worcester, NY: West Brothers Music.